THE MAGIC AND SCIENCE

OF

JEWELS AND STONES, VOL. II

BY

ISIDORE KOZMINSKY

Cassandra Press
San Rafael, CA 94915

CASSANDRA PRESS
P.O. BOX 868
SAN RAFAEL, CA 94915

ISBN 0-9615875-9-8

Library of Congress Catalogue Card Number 88-70720.

The use of the material described in this text is not meant to replace the services of a physician who should always be consulted for any condition requiring his or her aid.

TABLE OF CONTENTS

FOREWORD

Originally, this book was first written in 1922. The first volume in the rerelease of this text examines the use of gems in conjunction with astrology and the myths and stories associated with many stones. There is also a review of the rich folklore of gemstones from the Bible. Volume II of this work continues the comprehensive review of how people in many different cultures have used various gemstones in healing and spiritual activities. There is also a survey of the many gemstones referred to in the works of Shakespeare. In the middle ages the use of stones in healing and spiritual activities was much more common than is so today. Furthermore, there is a presentation of the chemical characteristics of gemstones.

It is hoped that in reading this book people will better understand how they can become empowered by using gemstones. Whether it is the wearing of a lapis lazuli necklace to improve one's speaking abilities or meditating with a rose quartz to open the heart, gemstones are very powerful vehicles to empower the individual.

As with the first volume, the original antiquated sytle of the text has been largely preserved. This has been done to maintain the character and authenticity of the book's content. Some words are spelled in the style that was common hundreds of years ago, while other passages have a Biblical style. And because Kozminsky lived in Australia a number of the words are spelled according to the style that is more common in England. The photographs in this book are all new because it was not possible to make good reproductions of the photographs in the original edition. Except for a brief comment on my two gem elixir books in the appendix , there are no footnotes concerning the many recent books about the healing and spiritual properties of gemstones. I felt that it would be better to preserve the original style and character of the book. Aside from adding new photographs, the other main change in the book is that it has been released in two volumes. Aside from these changes, the original book has been largely reproduced to reflect the content of the 1922 volume. I belief that many people will greatly enjoy and benefit from reading this well documented researched material.

Gurudas
San Rafael, Ca.
June, 1988

CHAPTER I

DICHROITE-IOLITE

Dichroite: Dioptase: Disthene: Emerald: Enstatite: Epidote: Essonite: Euclase: Flint, the Stone of Early Man: Its Use in Ancient Egypt: Ethiopian Arrows: The Elf Dart: Fairy Stone: Chias, the First to Prove the Flashing of Struck Flint: Its use in the Prevention of Nightmare: "Holey" Stones: Butler and the Hollow Flint: The Mara: The Garnet: Peculiarities: Dana's Classification: Succinite, A Harmony Charm: Grossularite, A Health Charm: Pyrope or Bohemian Garnet: Large Specimen in Saxon Regalia: Emperor Rudolph's Specimen: A Talisman of Friendship: Hope and Psychic Development: Spessartite, A Prayer Charm: Andradite, A Banisher of Unworthy Thoughts: Specimens Found Engraved with Angels' Names: Ouvarovite: Garnets Affect Magnetic Needle: Greenstone: Grossularite: Haematite: Sotacus's Classification of Haematite Varieties and Their Accredited Virtues: Dana's Classification: Pliny's Recommendation: Use in Ancient Times: Mummy's Headrest: Andreas Balvancensis' Idea: Stench Stone: Galen's Prescription: Hiddenite: Hornstone: Hyacinth: Virtues of the Hyacinth: The Jacinth Variety: Thomas De Cantempre's Description: Opinions of Leonardus and De Boodt: Francis Barrett's Comments: Observed Changes in the Stone: Avicenna's Comparison: The Hyacinth in the Garden of Peace and Amongst the Rosicrucian Jewels: Hydrophane: Hypersthene: Iolite.

DICHROITE: (see Iolite)

DIOPTASE: The name is derived from the Greek dia, through, and optomai, to see. This pretty emerald-green copper silicate was named in 1801 by Hauy, who found on looking through it cleavage directions. As the crystals are usually so small dioptase, which is of about the same degree of hardness as lapis lazuli, is seldom used in jewelry. According to ancient philosophy, dioptase would strengthen the sight of those who gazed upon it, and benefit if worn on the neck in throat troubles. Astrologically, dioptase is under the celestial Taurus.

DISTHENE: (see Kyanite)

EMERALD: (see Beryl)

ENSTATITE: Named from the Greek enstates, an opponent, because of its infusibility before the blowpipe and its resisting power against acids. It occurs in various colors—gray, brown, yellow, colorless, and chiefly green; hence it has been erroneously called the Green Garnet. The enstatite is a silicate of magnesium and is scarcely as hard as the opal, yet it is found with the diamond, hardest of stones. It is esteemed as a talisman in examinations, arguments, debates, and all contests in which the mind is employed. Enstatite is under the celestial Gemini.

EPIDOTE: This stone is named from the Greek epidosis, increase. It was first used by Hauy (*Mineralogie,* 1801), as "lit qui a recu un accroissement," but, writes Dr. Smith, "not on very precise crystallographical grounds." There are several varieties, chief among which is the Pistacite, or true Epidote, of a yellow-green color like the pistachio nut. The epidote is nearly as hard as the garnet. According to ancient philosophy, it may be used as a charm for fruit and cereal growers. The epidote is under the celestial Taurus.

ESSONITE: From the Greek esson; also, known as hessonite and more familiarly amongst jewelers as Cinnamon Stone. It is a garnet of the lime alumina order, of a reddish brown or cinnamon color and granular structure. This stone is often mistaken for hyacinth and other varieties of zircon with which it is found. It is regarded amongst ancient philosophers as a protective talisman for virgins born between August 24th and September 23rd. The essonite is a gem under the celestial Virgo.

EUCLASE: The name is derived from the Greek eu klasis, easily fractured. It is a silicate of aluminum and beryllium and is related to emerald. Westropp says, "The euclase is the same chemical composition as the emerald" (*Manual of Precious Stones*). It is a very rare and expensive mineral, glassy and extremely brittle. The euclase closely resembles the aquamarine in its varying shades of pale blue and pale green. Sometimes it is found quite colorless. It is frequently found with topaz and is of the hardness of the beryl. If the stone is to serve as a love talisman, it is advised that it be worn in the rough. The euclase is under the celestial Taurus.

FLINT:

"So stubborn flints their inward heart conceal
Till art and force th' unwilling sparks reveal."
Congreve to Dryden

Flint derives its name from the Greek plinthos, a brick. It has been written at various times as vlint, vlynt, flent, flend, flynd, flynt, and flynte. Flint is described as an "intermediate between quartz and opal, consisting almost entirely of silica with a little lime, oxide of iron, water, carbon and sometimes traces of organic matter." Mr. G. R. Porter says that flint is silica "in a state nearly approaching to purity (*Porcelain and Glass*, 1832). Today it is classed amongst the varieties of chalcedony and is found in various colors —grayish white, gray, black, light brown, red, and yellow. It is semi-translucent, breaking with a well-defined shell-like fracture. This mineral was extensively used by aboriginal man in making implements, weapons, magical instruments, and many finely worked specimens are still found in all parts of the world.

Mystery and magic are associated with the flint, which was used in ancient Egypt for fashioning scarabs and making the first incision in a dead body prior to embalming. The Ethiopian arrows noted by Herodotus were, as discovered, arrowheads of flint. Especially in Scotland and Ireland, the Elf Arrowhead or Elf Dart with a hole drilled through it was regarded as an effective talisman against poison, witchcraft, and the evil wishes of enemies.

Sir Edward Mackenzie Bart built his charming little story, "The Romance of the Elf Arrow," on these beliefs. Robert Gordon of Straloch, who wrote in the year 1654, relates that a friend of his was out riding on horseback when the top of his riding boot was struck by one of these fairy stones. In this case, there is no doubt that the horse's hoof caused the incident. But chance was not admitted by the old masters, who would regard the hoof of the horse as an instrument used by the mischievous fairies.

Pliny relates that Chias, being the first to demonstrate the fire flashing of struck flint, was given the name of Pyrodes. Aubrey states that it was an old custom to hang a flint with a hole in it on a string "to hinder the nightmare." "It is best of all, they say, hung about their necks, and a flint will do it that hath a hole in it. It is to prevent the nightmare, viz., the Hag, from riding their horses which will sometimes sweat at night. The flint thus hung does hinder it." Another writer, Grose, quoted in Brand's *Antiquities,* says, "A stone with a hole in it hung at the bed's head will prevent the nightmare. It is therefore called a Hag Stone from that disorder which is occasioned by a Hag or Witch sitting on the stomach of the party afflicted. It also prevents witches riding horses, for which purpose it is often tied to a stable key."

"Hang up Hooks and Sheers to scare
Hence the Hag that rides the mare."
                                                                    Herrick

These flints were called Holy or Holey Stones in the North of England, also Ephialtes stones, Night Mare, or Witch Riding Stones. Butler mentions the chasing away of evil spirits by hollow flint. The "Mare" of Night Mare is derived from the Saxon Mara, an incubus, which attacked during sleep, depriving the victim of movement and speech. The Mara, or Mare, is an order of vampires. Hebrew Maria is another evil spirit against which the flint is a charm. As a correspondent of flint, Emanuel Swedenborg gives Truth. Its connection with the ninth heavenly mansion is well defined. Flint is under the celestial Sagittarius.

GARNET:

"Without the aid of yonder golden globe
Lost were the garnet's lustre."
                                                                    Smart

The garnet derives its name from the Latin granatus, grain-like. Mr. King gives Granatici, from its resemblance to the scarlet pomegranate blossom. It is found written as garnet, gernet, garnette, garnat, garnet or garnat stone.

The mineral group passing under the general name of garnet exhibits some distinct peculiarities which, adopting the classification given by Professor James Dana, can be considered under three heads, as follows:

ALUMINA GARNET   IRON GARNET   CHROME GARNET

ALUMINA GARNET: The sesquioxide base is chiefly aluminum.

(a) **IRON ALUMINA GARNET:** Shades of color: Red, ruby red, hyacinth red, columbine red, and brownish red. Precious garnet is translucent, common garnet is not. Example: almandine or carbuncle. Astrologically, it is classed under the celestial Sagittarius.

(b) **LIME ALUMINA GARNET:** Shades of color: Pale green,

cinnamon, and amber. Examples: Essonite or Cinnamon Stone is cinnamon colored; grossularite (Latin grossularia, a gooseberry), is pale green; succinite (Latin succinum, amber), is the color of amber. The grossularite is a health talisman; the succinite a charm for securing harmony and success in dealing with employees. They are both under the celestial Virgo.

(c) **MAGNESIA ALUMINA GARNET:** Shades of color: Deep red changing to black and green. Example: Pyrope. Under the celestial Aquarius.

The pyrope, or Bohemian Garnet, derives its name from the Greek word puropos, fiery and was known to Pliny as apyroti. It is a stone of the same hardness as the beryl and is commonly called the "Cape Ruby," or the "Arizona Ruby." In the regalia of Saxony, set in the Order of the Golden Fleece, is a large pyrope, 468 1/2 carats in weight. That strange Emperor Rudolph II, under whose patronage Tycho and Kepler worked at the Rudolphine (Astronomical) Tables, is said by De Boodt to have possessed a specimen worth 45,000 thalers. One as big as a pigeon egg lies in the Green Vaults at Dresden. Large pyropes are, however, rare. Swedenborg corresponds pyrope to "good," and it is regarded as a talisman of faithfulness, stability, hope, happiness, and true friendship. Its influence is said to aid psychic development and occult understanding. It is a health stone and, in the East, is regarded as a banisher of plagues and poison. The stone changes color, it is said, when danger or mishap of any kind threatens the wearer.

(d) **MANGANESE ALUMINA GARNET:** Shades of color: Red, brownish red, and hyacinth red. Example: Spessartite, or spessartine. Under the celestial Virgo.

The spessartite obtains its name from Spessart in Germany. It is sometimes called the brown garnet, but is little used in jewelry. Spessartite is a prayer charm for the uplifted soul.

IRON GARNET: The sesquioxide base is chiefly iron.

LIME IRON GARNET: Shades of color: Various. Example: Andradite, named after the Portuguese mineralogist D'Andrada. In the variety called topazolite (so named after the topaz), the color is wine yellow, in jelletite it is green, and in melinite and pyreneite it is black or gray-black. The aplome (named by Hauy after the Greek word aploos, simple), is red. The kolophonite, named after kolophon in Ionia, is coarse, granular, resinous, and frequently iridescent. Green andradite has been termed the "Uralian Emerald" and the olivine (wrongly so-called under this head).

Brilliant specimens have been named demantoid by jewelers. A dark, almost black, andradite showing a gleam of red was much used in mourning jewelry. This is the stone which Leonardus said drove away pestilential airs and banished unworthy thoughts. It was a binding charm for friends. It protected from epidemics and the lightning stroke, and it lent favor to the desires of the native. Specimens have been found engraved with the names of angels in Chaldaic, Hebrew, Greek, and other ancient languages. It is under the celestial Aquarius.

CHROME GARNET: The sesquioxide base is chiefly chromium. Shades of color: Emerald green. Example: Ouvarovite, uvarovite or uwarowite, after the professor of that name of the late Russian Imperial Academy at Petrograd. The variety will not, like other varieties, yield to the blowpipe. It is a hard stone and few specimens large enough for cutting have been discovered. It is under the celestial Aquarius.

Many specimens of ancient engraved garnets have been found. Friction produces in the stone a positive order of electricity which has a perceptible effect on the magnetic needle.

GREENSTONE: (see Jade)

GROSSULARTIE: (see Garnet)

HAEMATITE:

> "The Haematite, named by the Greeks from blood,
> Benignant Nature formed for mortals' good."
> > Marbodus

The haematite obtains its name from the Greek haimatites, blood-like. It is a specular iron ore of reddish, brown, steely gray, and iron black colors. Commercially it is spelled hematite, though it is also written as hematite, emathites, and emathitis.

Sotacus, described by Pliny as one of the most ancient writers, classified five varieties of haematite, as follows:

1. Ethiopic, which he said was a remedy for burns and inflamed eyes. It is probable that this is the Ethiopian Stone, a hard species of flint (see under Flint).

2. Androdamus, or Conquerer of Man, which is given as a remedy for bilious attacks. This stone is described by Sotacus as "very black and heavy," and by Marbodus as "silvery white with the hardness of a diamond." It would seem that each writer is describing a different stone.

Sotacus' description would imply a species of iron stone; that of Marbodus may stand for a corundum or even a diamond. Man may be subdued by either the iron stone or the diamond.

3. Arabian, recommended for stomach troubles and burns.

4. Elatite, or when burned, melitite.

5. Mixed stone for eye troubles.

The varieties give by Professor James D. Dana are:

1. Specular iron, luster perfectly metallic.

2. Micaceous iron, structure foliated.

3. Red hematite, submetallic or unmetallic brownish red.

4. Red ochre, soft and earthy and often containing clay.

5. Red chalk, firmer and more compact than red ochre and of fine texture.

6. Jaspery clay iron, a hard, impure, siliceous, clay ore, having a brownish-red jaspery look and compactness.

7. Clay iron stone, the same as the last the color, but appearance less like jasper.

8. Lenticular argillaceous ore, an oolitic red ore consisting of small flattened grains.

9. Martite, hematite in octahedrons. It is supposed that martite is derived from the oxidation of magnetite.

Pliny says that haematites are found in mines and when burned have the color of minium. (Minium of today is our red lead of commerce, red oxide of lead.) He recommends it for affections of the bladder, for healing dangerous wounds and bites of serpents, and as a check to female disorders. It seems probable in these enumerations that he refers to loadstone (q. v.) for he says "the sanguine loadstone called haematite." The haematite and the loadstone were used in Babylon, Assyria, and other ancient lands as far back as 2,000 B.C. Amongst the specimens handled by the author was one notable haematite intaglio cylinder of very fine workmanship—a magistrate's seal of great antiquity. The ancient Egyptians generally selected haematite as a fitting pillow (Urs) for the head of the mummy to rest upon. On it were often cut verses from Chap. CLXVI of the *Book of the Dead*—the Per em Hru or Coming forth by Day.

An old 17th century writer, Andreas Balvacensis, advances the curious idea that the haematite was made of "dragon's blood," and Holme in his *Armoury* says that it is called a stench stone for its accredited virtue of stopping the flow of blood. Generally, the old writers of the Middle and later ages followed Galen in prescribing haematite for inflamed eyes and headaches. Galen was undoubtedly learned in the wisdom of the Egyptians and the old medical philosophies mentioned by Sotacus. Several modes of use are mentioned. One was to mix the powdered stone with honey and apply it to the eyelids; another was to rub the smoothed stone lightly over the lids. The kidney ore haematite, which has a strong metallic silky luster and is formed somewhat like a kidney, was recommended for external application over the region of that organ when ill conditions prevailed. This application of a Mars substance for the cure of a Venus affection is technically dealt with in works devoted to medical astrology, ancient and modern. Haematite is under the celestial Aries.

HIDDENITE: (see Spodumene)

HORNSTONE: Hornstone obtains its name from the Anglo-Saxon stan. It is a fragile variety of flint and is known in its more impure state as chert. It had some reputation as an eye stone in certain parts. Hornstone is regarded as being under the celestial Taurus.

HYACINTH:

> "The island of Sandareeb...containeth varieties of jacinths
> and different kinds of minerals."
> The 6th Voyage of Es-Sindabad of the Sea.

The name of this stone is derived from the youth Hyakinthos. It has been written at various times as hiacinth, hiacinthe, hyacint, hiacynth, hyacinthe, and hiacint. The true hyacinth, which is not to be confounded with the sapphire, the hyacinthus of the ancients, is a brilliant zircon (q.v.) of a transparent red or ruddy cinnamon color. It is found with a garnet of similar hue which is also called hyacinth but which shows structural differences and is classified under the name Essonite (q.v.). The peculiar granular nature of this hyacinth can be seen, even when cut, under an ordinary lens.

It is said in ancient story that Apollo caused the death of the lovely and beloved youth Hyakinthos when throwing his disc, and that from the blood which fell to the ground a lovely flower sprang. The myth symbolizes the fertility of nature and was celebrated by the festival Hyakinthia, which expresses the grief of Apollo over the precious life he had taken and the subsequent joy when the flower gave promise of the return of the slain one in harmony with nature's immortal moods. The gem hyacinth was considered a charm against bowel disorders, as a mental tonic, and as a strengthener of the mind against all kinds of temptation. It promised bountiful harvests to the farmer and filled the cornucopia of the Virgin Goddess.

The name jacinth, usually applied to the yellow variety of the gem, is a contraction of hyacinth, and appears as iacincte, iacynkte, iassink, jacounce, jagounce, jacinte, jacynct, and jacynth. Like all the zircon family, these stones are electric and attract fluff and exhibit phosphorescence. Thomas de Cantempre describes the jacinth as a stone of yellow color which protected the wearer from melancholy and poison, drawing to him the love of God and man. Leonardus said that it brought sleep to the tired brain and gave wisdom and protection in times of pestilence. De Boodt also recommends the gem as a cure for insomnia, advising that it be worn enclosed in a small bag of brown material suspended just over the solar plexus. Francis Barrett, in the section of his book devoted to natural magic says, "The jacinth also possesses virtue from the sun against poisons, pestilences, and pestiferous vapours. Likewise it renders the wearer pleasant and acceptable. Being simply held in the mouth it wonderfully cheers the heart and strengthens the mind."

So in ancient astrology these stones which are under the celestial Virgo, have these powers: wisdom and prudence, worldly gain, and wealth. It is said that so powerful were these gems of the zircon family that one wearing them could pass unharmed through places infected with fever and pestilence.

Similarly, it indicated the health of the wearer. Virgo is a sign of health and sickness. In old Polish pharmacies, a jacinth was kept set in a mount of silver, ready to be used to avert mortification in cases of accident. Mystic authors wrote that the jacinth grew dull when stormy weather was approaching and bright with the promise of fine weather. Cardanus said that in tempestuous weather the hyacinth assumes "the ruddy tint of a glowing coal." As an amulet against plague it was said to change color when touched by affected persons. Avicenna (Ibn Sina), the famous Arabian philosopher of the 10th century, compared the action of the jacinth with that of the magnet. Parcelsus says that it is distinctly under the government of the planet Mercury. Held against the forehead, it was reputed to give clearness of thought and calmness of mind. Swedenborg corresponds jacinth to "intelligence from spiritual love and in an opposite sense, intelligence from infernal love which is self-derived intelligence." To dream of hyacinth is interpreted as protection in approaching worries; to dream of jacinth indicates triumph. Jacinths are placed with almandines in the Dar as Salam, the Arabian Garden of Peace. Amongst the Rosicrucian jewels, the hyacinth represents the true knowledge of absolute love and the triumph over the crude elements of earthly understanding. These two zircon varieties are under the celestial Virgo.

HYDROPHANE: (see Opal)

HYPERSTHENE: The name is derived from the Greek hyper, over, and sthenos, strength. It is also written as hyperstene. It is a stone of the pyroxene group, a silicate of magnesium and iron. Its colors are brown-green, gray or green-black, and pinchbeck brown. Its hardness is about the hardness of lapis lazuli. The hypersthene is under the celestial Scorpio.

IOLITE: The iolite derives its name from the Greek ion, violet, and lithos, a stone. Hauy named it the Dichroite (dio, twice, chroa, color). It was known also as the cordierite, and more familiarly as the water sapphire. It is a silicate of alumina magnesia and protoxide of iron. It possesses extraordinary dichroism, the smoky blue and yellowish-gray being easily seen with the naked eye. This circumstance induced Hauy to name it dichroite. Viewed from two directions it presented different colors. These colors are shown to advantage in stones cut for ornament. In 1758, Sir James Hill wrote a *History of the Iolithos or Violet Stone*, a work now most difficult to obtain. The iolite is a stone of friendship and friendly help. It benefits the eyesight and is an aid to high thoughts. It was also written as yolite or iolithe. It is of about the hardness of quartz. The iolite is under the celestial Aquarius.

CHAPTER II

JACINTH-LODESTONE

Jacinth: Jade: Jargoon: Maturan Diamond: Jasper: The Lydian Stone of the Ancients: The Heliotrope or Bloodstone Variety: Thomas Nicols and Artificial Infusions: St. Isidore on the Jasper: Legend of the Cross: Number Five and the Stone of the Virgin: Rare Works in Jasper: Galenus on Its Virtues: The Anodyne Necklace: The Jasper Amulet of Nechepsos: The Wheel of Ezekiel: Jasper Sigils: Trallianus and the Jasper: Mottled Jasper, a Charm to Protect from Drowning: Zodiacal Reflections: The Stone of Victory: Van Helmont's Experiments: The Jasper Amongst the Jewels of the Rosicrucians: Jet: Kauri Gum: Kolophonite: Kunzite: Labrodorite: Lapis Lazuli: Colors and Names: Persian Lajward, Its Virtues: Its Place in the Book of the Dead: The Commandment Stones: Lapis Lazuli in China: Katherine II and Her Palace Room: A Stone of the Alchemists: Limonite: Lodestone: Pliny's Story of Its Discovery: How Termed By Titus Carus Lucretius: The Stone of Hercules: Legend of the Phoenicians: The Age of the Mariner's Compass: Construction of One by the Chinese Emperor Houangti: Pausanias and the Stone Image of Hercules: A Cramp Stone: A Divinatory Instrument: The Plan of Ptolemy Philadelphus: Professor Noad and the Power of the Lodestone: Barrett's "Antipathies": Story of Claudianus: Magnet and the Onion.

JACINTH: (see Hyacinth)

JADE: (see Nephrite)

JARGOON: The jargoon or jargon, by which name it is known in France, is derived from the Italian giacone. It is a grayish or smoky variety of the zircon, which so closely resembles the diamond that it is often sold by unscrupulous dealers for the more precious gem. In allusion to this, Sir A. H. Church, in his work on *Precious Stones* says, "The diamond and the jargoon do not improve or bring out each other's qualities for they have too many points in common." The jargoon, however, is nearly three degrees softer than the diamond and more easily injured. It is usually brilliant and rose-cut. At Matura in Ceylon, where it is found in fair quantities, it is frequently termed the "Maturan Diamond." The jargoon is frequently set as a talismanic charm against plagues and disease, for which purpose it was esteemed greatly in the Middle Ages, in the East, and in Europe. Worn on the little finger, set in a ring of silver, it was reputed to help the physician to correct diagnoses. When in doubt about a diagnosis, he held the stone against his forehead at a point between the eyes. The jargoon is under the celestial Virgo.

JASPER:

> "Jasper stone signifies the divine truth of the Word in its literal sense, translucent from the divine truth in its spiritual sense."
>
> Swedenborg

Jasper derives its name from the Hebrew yashpheh, Greek iaspis, Arabic yasb. It is found written as jasp, japre, iaspere, and iaspar. It is a hard siliceous mineral of dark, dull colors, chiefly red, green, yellow, and black. In the variety termed riband, the mixed and striped colors form in concentric irregular zones. Ruin jasper occurs in darker shades of browns and yellows, giving the appearance of venerable ruins. The lapis lydius (the Lydian Stone of the ancients) or our basanite, commonly known as touchstone, is a velvety black, flinty jasper. It is used as much today as ever it was for ascertaining the fineness and quality of gold and precious metals. Bacon said, "Gold is tried by the touchstone and men by gold."

Jasper's connection with Mercury is shown in the Greek story of the transformation of the betrayer Battus into touchstone by God. The heliotrope, or so-called bloodstone, variety is green with spots of red. Pliny enumerates ten varieties, giving preference to the purple and rose-colored ones. Marbodus, in the *Lapidarium*, writes of 17 species all differing in color, the best of all being the bright translucent green. The jasper was held in high favor by the ancients, and Babylonian seals as old as 1,000 years before the Christian era have been found. The Thet, or Buckle, of Isis was made chiefly of jasper. In those times, the stone was found in quantities in the vicinity of the historic town of On, or Heliopolis.

Thomas Nicols, writing in the 17th century, protests that the Egyptians knew how to infuse artificial colors into this gem: "It is ascribed by way of glory to the King of Egypt that the first adulteration of jasper by tincture was from him, but the glory of this praise, if I be not mistaken, doth even become his shame." St. Isidore of Seville (16th of the green jasper as "shining with the greenness of glory." This variety—commonly known as bloodstone because it is spotted with red specks resembling drops of blood—is regarded as an essentially religious substance, and is associated with the old Easter ceremonies.

There is an old legend that drops of blood from the five wounds of the dying Christ fell on the green jasper lying at the foot of the Cross at the Crucifixion, and these drops were forever impregnated in the stone. Five is the number which in mystic writings is identified with the planet Mercury. The significance of the blood of the Son of the Virgin in the stone of the Virgin will be understood by those who search for truth beneath the mantle of parable. Mr. William Jones, in *Finger Ring Lore*, gives an illustration of a Christian octagonal-shaped ring of the 3rd or 4th century, set with a red jasper in which is cut in intaglio a shepherd and his flocks. The import of this is clear enough. A jasper bust of Christ in which the red spots are so manipulated by the skillful artist as to represent drops of blood is mentioned by Professor James Dana as being in the royal collection at Paris.

"Some indeed assert," writes Claudius Galenus, the famous physician of the second Christian century, "that a virtue such as is possessed by the green jasper which benefits the chest and mouth of the stomach if tied upon it, is inherent in precious stones. I have had ample experience having made a necklace out of such gems (jaspers), and hung it round the neck, descending so low that the stones might touch the mouth of the stomach, and they appeared to be of no less service than if they had been engraved in the way laid down by King Nechepsos." This is the famous anodyne necklace so valued, especially in England, and the source of which the distinguished physician Dr. William Cullen ascribes to Galenus.

Several books are credited to King Nechepsos (circa 600 B.C.). Galenus alludes to this King's jasper amulet which took the form of a rayed dragon. This dragon form symbolizes the mystery of the three zodiacal signs—Virgo, Libra, and Scorpio—known to students of Rosicrucian philosophy as the Wheel of Ezekiel and personified in Pallas Athene or Minerva, the embodiment of wisdom, sympathy, and strength. Galenus carried as his talismanic gem, a jasper engraved with a man carrying a bundle of herbs, as an aid to his judgment in indicating various diseases— a power long ascribed to stones under the celestial Virgo. A similar sigil is given by the ancient Israelitish Rabbi Chael: "A man with broad shoulders and thick loins, standing and holding in his right hand a bundle of herbs engraved on a green jasper is good against fevers, and if a physician carries it about with him it will give him skill in distinguishing diseases and knowing the proper remedies. It is also good for hemorrhoids and quickly stops the flow of blood." The same authority recommends for good luck in buying and selling "Aquarius cut on a green jasper," which is also termed "a stone of good counsel for traders." (All trade is under Mercury, the ruler in astrology of the signs Gemini and Virgo.) A man's head facing and a bird holding a leaf in its beak, cut in jasper, was held to give riches and favor; a hare cut in jasper protected from evil spiritual forces.

The green jasper, as before stated, was also known as the heliotropion (heliotrope), a word derived from Greek helios, the sun, and tropos, a turn—probably in allusion to the planet Mercury which turns nearest the Sun. It is stated that if this stone were placed in water it would reflect the blood-red disc of the sun, and if held before the eyes it would assist in the observation of the solar and lunar eclipses. Trallianus, a 6th century philosopher, recommends the jasper for pains of an acute nature in the stomach or bowels—a use for which it was especially esteemed by all ancient scholars. Mottled jasper was worn to protect from death by drowning, or from death while on or near the water. This presents one of the many instances of what astrologers term "sign reflection," for the water sign of the Fishes (Pisces) is opposite to the earth sign Virgo and serves as an apt illustration of antipathetic action.

Another virtue ascribed to jasper was the calming of uneasy minds and the securing of victory in battle. In this latter connection, Cardanus, a physician, philosopher, and astrologer of the 16th century, says that it has action on the feelings, causing something akin to timidity which induces caution and the evading of needless risks—a distinctly mercurial attribute. De Boodt advises the wearing of jasper to check hemorrhage and relieve stomach pains. The stomach was regarded as the seat of the soul by the remarkable Baptista van Helmont. Deleuze credits him with "creating epochs in the histories of medicine and physiology, and of first giving the name of 'gas' to aerial fluids," adding that without him, "it is probable that steel would have given no new impulse to science."

Van Helmont writes, "In the pit of the stomach there is a more powerful sensation than even in the eye or in the fingers. The stomach often will not tolerate a hand to be laid upon it because there is there the most acute and positive feeling which at other times is only perceived in the fingers." For purposes of experiment Van Helmont touched a root of aconite with the tip of his tongue—a risky action—taking care, however, not to swallow any of it. "Immediately," he says, "my head seemed tied tightly with a string and soon after there happened to me a singular circumstance such as I had never before experienced. I observed with astonishment that I no longer felt and thought with the head but with the region of the stomach, as if consciousness had now taken up its seat there. Terrified by this unusual phenomenon, I asked myself and enquired unto myself carefully, but I only became more convinced that my power of perception had become greater and more comprehensive. This intellectual clearness was associated with great pleasure. I did not sleep, nor did I dream. I had occasionally had ecstasics but these had nothing in common with this condition of the stomach in which it thought and felt and almost excluded all co-operation of the head. This state continued for two hours after which I had some dizziness."

Van Helmont writes of the "Sun tissue" in the region of the stomach which from the earliest recorded times has been identified with the zodiacal Virgo around which so many myths, parables, and legends cluster. Jasper is associated with this part of the body of man. To dream of it is said to symbolize love's faithfulness known to the mind before the heart:

"Love looks not with the eyes but with the mind,
And therefore is Dan Cupid painted blind."

Amongst the symbolic jewels of the Rosicrucians this stone was regarded as the center stone of the vibrations of light and of its penetrating diffusions. All varieties of jasper are under the celestial Virgo.

JET:

"Your lustre too'll draw courtship to you as a iet (jet) doth straws."
Ben Jonson

The name jet is derived from the Greek gagates from Gagas, a river in Syria. It is also written as jesstone, and jeetstone. Dr. Murray gives the following forms: gete, geet, get, geete, geyte, geitt, gett, gette, geytt, gate, giette, geate, ieet, iete, ieit, ieate, iet, jeat, jett, and jette. It is a variety of coal resembling cannel coal, but harder, of deeper color, and with a higher degree of luster. Pliny writes that "Gagates is a stone so-called from Gages, the name of a town and river in Lycia." When burned it gives out a sulphurous smell which, according to the Venerable Bede (7th century), drove away serpents. Its virtue was esteemed in cases of hysteria, in detecting epileptic tendencies, and in loss of virginity. A decoction of jet in wine was esteemed as a cure for toothache, and in combination with wax, it was used in cases of scrofula.

Magicians, it is said, make use of gagates in the practice of what is known as "Axinomancy"—a form of magic in which a piece of jet is placed on a red-hot axe—prophesying events according to the burning of the substance. Jet is highly electrical and will attract fluff in the same way as amber does, hence it was known as black amber, especially in the 16th century, by the people of the Baltic coast. It was much used in magical ceremonies, especially those in connection with the dead, as a charm against evil magic, spells, and envy and as a cure for dropsy, colds, chills, and loss of hair. The fumes from burning jet are no doubt very relieving in what is commonly known as cold in the head, the action being homeopathic in this case, as such discomforts are saturnine and the employment of jet is the employment of a saturnine substance for removing a saturnine affliction.

The use of jet for rosaries is noted by Cardan. It cooled the passions and protected the wearer against evil influences. Its fumes were considered potent in female disorders. Boetius said it protected the wearer against nightmares and night terrors. Mr. King mentions the discovery of a number of jet ornaments at Cologne in 1846. These were believed to have belonged to the ancient priestesses of Cybele, or Rhea, the goddess of the mountain-forests and caves of the earth. Her worship was wild and weird. Her votaries rushed through the trees in the darkness of the night, with torches ablaze fighting and wounding each other to the accompaniment of screeching pipes, clashing cymbals, and the mad uproar of drunken song. Cybele was associated as a mountain goddess with the forest-god Pan, the goat-god, who is identified with the zodiacal Capricornus, and jet was used in her worship.

Jet was regarded as a banisher of melancholia and a protective badge for travelers. To dream of it was said to signify sadness. As a shield against the bites of serpents, it was advised that powdered jet be taken and mixed with the marrow of a stag. To many writers this has seemed ridiculous, but beneath the surface the true meaning may be detected. Astrologically, jet is under the zodiacal Capricorn and the planet Saturn, the stag is under Gemini and the planet Mercury. The marrow of the stag is ruled by Venus and in this case signifies the essence supreme. The serpent is under the planet Mars. Interpreted, this symbolic passage would read: use wisdom and caution (jet), knowledge (stag), and love (marrow); then wilt thou overcome, subdue, and defeat the lower self (serpent) and the sting of sin. Crypts of this kind were very frequently employed by Hermetic brotherhoods for conveying their teachings to each other. The use of parables, secret signs, tokens, and symbols was the real method of conveying truths employed by the ancient masters. By this means, concentration was impelled and the soul prepared to receive great truths.

KAURI GUM:

"As some tall Kauri soars in lonely pride."
                              Renwick

Kauri obtains its name from the Maoris and appears in various forms: kowrie, cowry, courie, and coudie. It is gum of a light amber color which has exuded from the kauri pine (*Dammara Australis*), a species of Dammar growing in New Zealand. The gum is obtained by digging over spots where the trees once grew, and it is found sometimes in lumps the size of a football. Kauri gum is electric and much softer and less durable than amber. It has been suggested as a useful substitute for amber in throat troubles, asthma, hay fever, and glandular swellings. It is under the celestial Taurus.

KOLOPHONITE: (see Garnet)

KUNZITE: (see Spodumene)

KYANITE: Kyanite derives its name from the Greek kuanos, blue. It is also written as cyanite and, because of its unequalled hardness, disthene (twice strong). White specimens are termed rhoetizite. Chemically, kyanite harmonizes with andalusite for both are silicates of aluminum, but as Dr. Smith writes, "Points of difference show how large a share the molecular grouping has in determining the aspect of crystallized substances." Usually kyanite is found in long, thin, blade-like crystals and more rarely in short, full crystals. Its colors are light blue, blue and white, white, gray-green and, more rarely, black. Its hardness varies from 5 to a little over 7 in Mohs' scale. When cut, the blue variety resembles the light sapphire, although it cannot display the same brilliancy. The stone is, however, very little employed in jewelry. The peculiarities of kyanite place it under the celestial Aquarius.

LABRADORITE:

"The beautiful opalised kind of felspar called Labrador stone."
                                                          Pinkerton

Also written labrador, this is an opalescent gray-blue felspar of extraordinary gleam, often reflecting green, yellow, and red. It obtains its name from the place of its origin, as it was first found at St. Paul Island off the coast of Labrador by Moravian missionaries in 1770. Specimens have also been found in stones of meteoric origin. The stone is effective and might with advantage be more extensively used in jewelry. Its hardness is the same as opal. Labradorite is under the celestial Aquarius.

LAPIS LAZULI:

"The appearance of the Lord's divine sphere in the spiritual Heavens."
Swedenborg

Lapis lazuli derives its name from the Latin word lapis, a stone, and the Arabic azul, blue. It has been variously written as zumemo lazuli, zemech lazarilli, stellatus, lapis lazary, lapis coelestus, the azure gem, the Armenian stone, and lapis lazari. Its composition includes for the greater part silica and alumina, with soda, lime, iron, sulphuric acid, sulphur, chlorine, and water. It is assumed to be a product of contact metamorphism, and is described by Pliny as "opaque and sprinkled with specks of gold" (yellow pyrites). It is found in Persia, Tartary, China, Tibet, and Siberia. Badakhshan, or Budukhshan, in Central Asia is famous for its lapis lazuli mines in which, it is recorded, the rock is split with the help of fire. The stone is often found in tints of green, red, violet, or colorless, but these may be termed varieties. The miners of Budukhshan call the blue lapis "Nili," the sky-blue "Asmani," and the blue-green tints "Sabzi." Some of the finest lajward (lapis lazuli) is sent from the Persian markets whence formerly specimens of rare beauty were exposed for sale at the fairs of Nijni-Novgorod. From very remote times, Persia supplied the ancient world with the greatest quantities of lajward.

The "sapphirus" of old is the lapis lazuli of today, and it is recommended that the 26th chapter of the *Book of the Dead* should be recited before a deific figure cut from this stone. As early as 1500 years before Christ, we have a record that the lapis lazuli placed on the neck of a sick child reduced fever. Many Egyptian priests wore images formed from the stone, which was regarded as an emblem of the heavens. Epiphanius, Bishop of Constantia in Cyprus, at the latter part of the 4th century, quotes from older sources the tradition that the tables of the Law of Moses were written on two blocks of lapis lazuli, which is identified as the eleventh stone of the magic Breastplate. In the ceremonies of the Temple of Heaven in China, ornaments of Liu-Li (lapis lazuli) were used, and the Chinese sacred writings record how at one time the priest-kings bore it as an offering to the Lord of the Universe.

In accordance with the desire of Catherine II of Russia, her favorite room in the Zarskoe Selo palace was adorned with lapis lazuli, symbolic of the country she governed, and amber, as a symbol of herself. The ancient Greeks and Romans considered a piece of lapis lazuli—the stone of Heaven—as the most fitting distinction to bestow for personal bravery. It was regarded as a true stone of friendship and of the affection arising from friendship. Ancient physicians regarded this gem as of potent value in eye troubles, one old prescription advising that a specimen be placed in a bowl of pure water, warm but not hot, for some few minutes, and then that the eye affected be bathed in the water.

The stone was also valued if placed, just warm, on swellings or seats of pain. It was also regarded as a cure for ague, melancholia, disorders of the blood, neuralgic affections, and spasmodic action. As a talisman, it was worn to protect against injuries, especially to the ankles, to attract friends, gain favors, and realize hopes. Lapis lazuli was used by many of the old alchemists in special work of an esoteric nature. It is frequently alluded to as the Stone of Heaven in which the stars are held. It is under the zodiacal Aquarius.

LIMONITE: This stone was named limonite by Professor Hausmann in 1813 from the Greek word leimon, a meadow. It is a species of brown haematite (scarcely as hard as the opal). According to Professor Dana, limonite appears to have been the result in all cases of the decomposition of other iron-bearing rocks or minerals. It is under the celestial Aries.

LODESTONE:

"The magnet weds the steel, the secret rites
Nature attends and th' heavenly pair unites."
Claudianus of Alexandra

The lodestone, which is also written though not so correctly, loadstone, obtains its name from the Anglo-Saxon lad a course, lithan, to lead, and stan. Another form is Lodysshestone, the stone that shows the way. It is also known as magnetite or the ancient magnet, from the Greek Magnes. The lodestone or magnetite is a black iron ore of high magnetic quality, and this peculiar attracting force is said to have first indicated what we now term magnetism. According to Pliny, a Greek shepherd— Magnes, by name—while tending his sheep on Mount Ida, found pieces of lodestone clinging to the ferrule of his shepherd's staff. Titus Carus Lucretius, in his great philosophical work, *De Rerum Natura* (about 55 B.C.), calls magnetite the magnesium stone, which he said obtained its name from Magnesia, a town in Thessaly.

Another name applied to this stone is siderit, but its best known appellation in the ancient world was heraclion, or stone of Hercules. It is interesting to recall the legend of the old Phoenician mariners, which tells that Hercules, admiring their daring and skill, desired to help them in the science of navigation. For this purpose he obtained from Helios a cup of

Heraclion which always turned to the North. This seems to indicate that the mariners' compass is of an older date than the 11th century; indeed, the Chinese assert that, in the year 2634 B.C., the Emperor Houangti first constructed a magnetic compass. The Greek traveler and historian Pausanias, in his *Helbados Periegesis* published in the second century, writes of the rough stone image of Hercules in the Temple at Hyettos, which the sick came but to touch in order to be healed of their disorders.

As a stone of healing the lodestone was highly esteemed as a cure for gout, rheumatism, cramp, and disorders which frequently yield to treatment wherein iron is employed. It was used during childbirth and in diseases of the generative organs. Finely powdered and mixed with oil or grease, it was regarded by ancient writers as a preventive of or cure for baldness. In the Orphic Lythica, it is stated that if this stone was held to the head, voices of the gods could be heard, heavenly knowledge gained, and divine things seen. It also states that one should sit alone in earnest meditation asking the celestial powers for guidance or help in some particular trouble, when the reply flowing through the stone would be quickly sensed and understood by the sincere petitioner.

A woman's moral character was said to be betrayed by lodestone which endowed strength, will, and the ability to look into the future. It was also carried as a charm to protect against shipwreck. It is related that, after the death of his sister-wife Arsinoe, Ptolemy II (Philadelphus), with his architect Dinochares planned a temple to be built of lodestone in order that her iron statue would be held for ever in suspension, seemingly in space, but his death defeated the plan.

In referring to the power of lodestones Professor Noad (*Electricity*) states, "The smallest stones have greater attractive force in proportion to their size than the larger ones." Francis Barrett, under the heading of *Antipathies,* writes that a diamond disagrees with a lodestone and being present suffers no iron to be drawn to the lodestone. However, it is as a lovers' token that the lodestone is most extolled; it is often found set in lovers' rings of the Middle Ages. Claudianus, in his *Idyl* published in the latter part of the 4th century, gives a record of a temple wherein was a statue of Venus in lodestone and another of Mars in iron—symbols of the attraction of the wife for the husband and of the husband for the wife. There is an old belief that the magnet was affected by the onion, and in this connection the following extract from *Notes and Queries*, December, 1917, is interesting: "The notorious Count de Benyowsky at the end of Chapter III of his *Memoirs and Travels* mentions the strategem which he tried at sea to falsify the compass by the use of iron and garlic. I now find that in the 17th century the belief actually prevailed in England that an onion would destroy the power of the magnet. Thus, Sir John Pettus of

Kent, after describing his visit as a youth to the lead mines of Derbyshire in company with Sir Thomas Bendish, says that having magnetized the blade of his knife and hearing that contact with an onion would utterly destroy that power, he preferred to believe rather than risk losing his magnet. The passage occurs in a rambling note on *Mineralls* in the second part of his *Fleta Minor*." It might be considered in connection with such stories that the onion as well as the lodestone is of the zodiacal Scorpio. To dream of the lodestone warns of subtle dealings and contentions. It is under the celestial Scorpion.

Garnet

CHAPTER III

MALACHITE-NEPHRITE

Malachite: Rosicrucian Symbol of Eternal Spring: Used in Antique Cameos and Intaglios: Virtues: A Sleep Stone: Marble, the Stone of Statues: Varieties: Emblem of Immortality: The Symbol of Mercury: The Image of Silenus: Meerschaum: Kavol Kowates Makes a Meerschaum Pipe: Melanite: Moonstone or Ceylon Opal: Indian Beliefs: Stone of Prophecy and Love: Specimen of Pope Leo X: Moss Agate: An Emblem of Resurrection: Orpheus' Advice: Mother of Emerald: Mother of Pearl: Nacre: Emblem of Women: Custom of the West Australian Native: Nephrite: Lapis Nephriticus or Kidney Stone: Sir Walter Raleigh's Description: Jade and Jadeite: Camphor Jade: Burmese Jade: Nephrite Charms: Chinese and Jade: Find Near Peking: The Nine Accomplishments and the Five Cardinal Virtues: Jade as a Preventive of Decay: Musical Jade Stones: The Lunar Festivals: Jade of the North, South, East, and West: Its Healing Virtues: Buddha's Footmark: Symbol of Rulership: Adadu-Nephros or Kidney of Adonis: The Six Varieties of the Maoris: The Hei Tiki: The Tahunga Stone and the Mere or Pattoo Pattoo: Damour's Chloromelanite: Pate De Riz: Pink Jade: Ionan Jade: The Hysteria Stone at the New York Museum of Natural History.

MALACHITE:

> "Melochites is a grene stone lyke to Smaragdus and
> hath that name of the colour of Malawes."
> Trevisa

The malachite derives its name from the Greek malache, marsh mallow, from its resemblance to the soft green leaves of this plant. It is variously written as melochite and malachquit. It is a green carbonate of copper which comes to us through the ages as a symbol of children and of the child of the year—eternal Spring. It has been confused with the Molochite of Pliny, but it is more likely the smaragdus medicus, as identified by Mr. King, and the chrysocolla of Theophrastus. In Rosicrucian philosophy, malachite was the symbol of the vernal equinox and the arising of the spiritual man. Malachite and azurite have been found together in single specimens. Malachite is much employed for decorative purposes by the Russians, who have produced some excellent works of art in this material. It was greatly favored by the Egyptians and antique cameos and intaglios have been frequently found patinated by the hard hand of age.

The virtues ascribed to this stone are many. It strengthens the stomach, head, and kidneys; prevents vertigo and rupture; and saves the wearer from evil magic, seduction, falls, and accidents. The Egyptians held it to be efficacious in cholera and rheumatism. It was said to bestow strength on children, to aid them during dentition, and to ward off convulsions, all harm, witchcraft, and the evil eye. Some old writers give directions for swallowing powdered malachite, especially for cardiac affections—a practice dangerous and undesirable. The action of stones and gems is subtle, and the intense vibratory action is so gentle as to be usually quite unfelt by the material senses. Powdering a specimen disturbs the cohesive molecules and deprives them of their insidious action. A stone multiplies from without, and by the laws of correspondence, its action on man is always from external to internal.

The malachite was also called the sleep stone, from its reputation of charming the wearer to sleep. It was also regarded as a protection from lightning. Massive malachite bears a close resemblance to the kidneys in the human body. It is under the zodiacal Libra.

MARBLE:

"And the cold marble leapt to life, a god."
Milman

Marble derives its name from the Latin marmor, cognate with the Greek marmoros, from marmairo, to sparkle. It has been variously written in England as marbre, marbyr, marbel, marbal, marboll, marbelle, merbyl, marbill, marbyll, marbull, and marbell. It is carbonate of lime, pure when the color is white; and of various shades of color when combined with oxide of iron and other substances. The marble favored by the ancients was the parian which is finely granular, waxy when polished, and lasting. The beautiful Venus de Medici and other exquisite Greek statues were formed of parian. Another favorite variety was the more finely grained and whiter marble of pentelicus from which the Parthenon was built. The Pyramid of Cheops and other famous structures of the kind were built of a variety known as nummilitic limestone, which is composed of numerous disk-shaped fossils called nummilites.

Portor is a deep black Genoese marble with yellow veinings. The deep black marble of antiquity is known as nero-antico; rosso antico is a deep blood-red besprinkled with minute white marks; verde antico is a misty green; giallo antico is a deep yellow with yellow or black rings. Carrara marble is often used by modern sculptors and was well-known to the ancients; it is a fine-grained, pure white marble traversed by gray veins. Pure white marble was an emblem of purity and has always been regarded as fitting for tombstones and other sepulchral monuments.

As an emblem of immortality marble is expressed by the triform symbol of the planet Mercury (the cross, the circle, and the crescent), with which is associated the Christ resurrection in Christian mysticism. Amongst Rosicrucian students, the cross is symbolical of the pain of matter, for on it matter is fixed: the circle is the ascent of the soul, which is above matter and never ending; the semi-circle, which surmounts the whole, is the spirit which is over all everlastingly. Evidence of the old custom still followed in many countries of placing pieces of white marble in the grave with dead bodies was some few years ago brought to light in Ireland. Dr. Holland's translations from Pliny record "a strange thing of the quarries of the island Paros, namely, that in one quarter thereof there was a vein of marble found which when it was cloven in twaine with wedges shewed naturally within the true image and perfect portraiture of Silenus imprinted on it." All marble is under the celestial Gemini.

MARCASITE: (see Pyrite)

MEERSCHAUM:

"A meerschaum pipe nearly black with smoking is considered a treasure."
                    J. Nott, Dekker's *Gull's Horn Book*

Meerschaum obtains it name from the German meer, sea, and schaum, foam, which is, according to Dr. Murray, a literal translation of the Persian kef-i-darya, foam of the sea. It is also called keffekill and kiffekiefe, which have been credited with meaning the "earth of the town of Keffe or Kaffe," the Crimean town whence it is exported. Its technical name is sepiolite, and its various forms are given as myrsen, meershaum, meerchum, mereschaum, merschaum, and meerschaum. It is a hydrous silicate of magnesia, extremely soft and light, smooth to the touch and colored white, gray-white, yellow, and sometimes pinkish. Kirwan, the mineralogist who wrote in the latter part of the 18th century, says, "Kefferkill or myrsen is said, when recently dug, to be of a yellow colour and as tenacious as cheese or wax." It is well-known that the Tartars use newly dug meerschaum as we use soap, on account of its excellent lather. The peasantry at one time really believed it to be the petrified foam of the sea.

The meerschaum is included amongst the galactites or milk stones. On account of its lightness, Kavol Kowates, a Hungarian shoemaker skilled in wood carving and metal work, first fashioned it into a smoking pipe. Kowates lived in the old town of Pestk, and the pipe now rests in the museum of that town. The piece of meerschaum from which Kowates made his pipe was brought to Hungary by his patron Count Andrassy on his return from a diplomatic mission to Turkey. The meerschaum is under the celestial Gemini.

MELANITE: (see Garnet)

MOONSTONE:

> "Soon as the evening shades prevail,
>   The Moon takes up the wondrous tale.
>   And nightly to the listening earth
>   Repeats the story of her birth."
>   Addison

The moonstone is an orthoclase feldspar of the opalescent variety of adularia, of a pearly moonlike luster—hence the name Stone of the Moon. It appears under the forms of moona, mone, mon, mowne, moone, moyne, mione, mune, and muni. It is known in France as Pierre de la Lune. Its abundance in Ceylon has earned for it the name of Ceylon Opal. The Indians call it Candra Kanta, according to them, it grows under the rays of the moon and absorbs, in the process of formation an atmospheric ether which impregnates it with peculiar occult and magical properties. These properties once infused into the stone never leave it. They are said to have a remarkable effect on the psychic nature of man, enabling him to prophesy—according to Leonardus—in the waning of the moon and to love in the waxing.

The natives of Ceylon have a story that every thirty-seventh year, moonstones of opalescent blue are, by the influence of the moon, hurled on the island shore by the waves. Pliny says that in the stone an image of the moon is impressed, which waxes and wanes in harmony with the luminary. It is related that Pope Leo X possessed a wonderful specimen which, obscure and dull when the moon was old, increased in brilliance as that orb grew from new to full. It is recommended that, in order to know the future and to obtain spiritual guidance, a moonstone be held in the mouth under a waning moon. It is also necessary to be quite alone and to send out a mental prayer to the angel Gabriel (angel of the Moon) asking help by God's grace.

The moonstone was considered as a charm against cancer, dropsy, and affections of a watery nature. In fever, if applied to the temples, it reduced the temperature and protected the patient. It also cooled heated imaginations and protected against moonstrokes and lunacy. The moonstone is said to protect the wearer from danger on the ocean and to give good fortune while traveling. As a symbol it signifies hope, and as a dream symbol it indicates traveling and health—good when the stone is bright and clear, and bad when it is dark and lusterless. It is under the celestial Cancer.

MOSS AGATE or MOCHA STONE:

"Whilst on that agate which dark Indians praise
The woods arise, the sylvan monster strays."
Marbodus

The mocha stone is said to have obtained its name from the Arabian city of Mocha whence it was exported. It has been written in various ways: mocus, mocoe, mocoa, mochoe, mochoa, mocha, and mocho. It is called Piedra de Moca in Spain, Pierre de Mocka in France, and Mokkastein in Germany. The mocha stone is called dendritic because of the plant and moss-like infiltrations exhibited. These are like frost crystals often formed by the magic hand of nature, and also by plants held in hollows wherein the siliceous mineral was composed. The mocha stone, besides being called moss agate, is also called tree agate in common with silicified trees in which the original structural details are accurately preserved. Remarkable pictures formed by nature in the agate have already been noticed. Pliny hints at the employment of artifice in the production of many of these stones, and the secret was long a cherished knowledge of the Italian workers in gems. Early in the 19th century, however, some German scientists obtained possession of the secret and within the past few years artificial productions from Oberstein have reached the gem mar-

The mocha stone was accounted a most fortunate stone. It is associated with the influences of the planet Venus and was always noted as a sign of fertility. For this reason, farmers tied specimens to their fruit trees, to the harness of their horses, and to the horns of their cattle. In the early 19th century, it was highly esteemed in Europe and in England was especially used for luck rings. It was often surrounded with rubies (stones of the sun) and was used for mourning jewelry as an emblem of the resurrection and of the eternal life which alone is permanently manifest throughout nature. Orpheus advises that to secure the smiles of the gods a piece of the stone should be worn, and that the ploughman carrying it would receive heavenly bounty. It was greatly esteemed by physicians and apothecaries as a base on which to prepare their medicines. As a symbol it stood for good health and long life and to dream of it meant an increase of possessions. It is under the celestial Taurus.

MOTHER OF EMERALD: (see Plasma)

MOTHER OF PEARL: (see Nacre)

NACRE:

> "'Tis a valley paved with golden sands,
>   With pearls and nacre shells."
>   *Sylvester* (1605), Trans. Du Bartas

Nacre, or Mother of Pearl, is the inner layer of various molluscs and is more particularly applied to the meleagrina margaritifera, or large oyster shell, in which the precious pearl is formed. The French call it mere perle, and it is found written as moder perl, mother perle, mother pearle. Nacre is said to have derived its name from the Persian word nigar, painting, because of the iridescent colors displayed. Dr. Murray, although remarking on its probable Oriental origin, regards its derivation as uncertain. Various forms are noted, such as: nackre, nacker, nakre, and naker. There is no doubt of its antique application. Hoole in 1658 wrote that "the oyster affordeth sweet meat—the nacre pearls."

Mythologically, the mother of pearl shell is symbolical of Latona or Leto, "goddess of the dark night," mother of the Sun god Apollo and the Moon goddess Artemis or Diana. She, as ancient story tells, while fleeing from the fury of Hera, Queen of Heaven, reached an island rock, driven about by restless waves, which when solidly fixed by Neptune became the famous island of the Aegean Sea—Delos. Here were born the radiant twins Apollo and Artemis in a flood of golden light, while the sacred swans encircled the island seven times. The golden light, so powerful at this event, is the light which at conjunction (new moon) blends with the silvery light of the night orb.

The pearl shell, like its child the pearl, is always associated with female life, which in astrophilosophy is moon-ruled. The natives of Western Australia, hidden in the bushes, charmed women by the aid of the reflected light from the shell of the mother of pearl. These big shells are thick, flat, and roundish in size often as much as a foot in diameter. The two varieties are known as black-lipped and silver-lipped, and within them rests the protected pearl. The pearl shell is greatly in demand for the manufacture of many and varied articles of commerce. It is under the celestial Cancer—the mansion of the moon and the sign of the deep ocean.

NEPHRITE:

> "Many of the Indians wore pieces of Greenstone round their necks
> which were transparent and resembled an emerald. These being
> examined, appeared to be a species of nephrite stone."
>
> Cook's *Voyages,* 1790

In ancient times, the minerals comprising or included in this important group were commonly known by the name lapis nephriticus, or kidney stone. From this name in the 18th century. Dr. A. G. Werner suggested the term nephrite. To the nephrite varieties the general term jade is universally applied. The name occurs in old writings as jad or jadde, and is derived from the Spanish hijada, kidney. Sir Walter Raleigh in 1595 wrote of this "kinde of stones which the Spaniards call piedras hijadas and we use for spleene stones." Chemically the species included under the name "jade" are not the same, the nephrite jade being a silicate of lime and magnesia and the jadeite a silicate of sodium and alumina, but the modern scientist in common with the ancient scientist binds them together under the one denomination—kidney stone.

In the 19th century, Professor A. Damour demonstrated the chemical difference between jade and jadeite. The well-known Camphor Jade of China is a white jadeite, some specimens containing certain percentages of chromium exhibiting those apple-green patches so highly praised by gem collectors. Burmese jade, known as Chauk-Sen (which since the 13th century has been principally exported to China), is chiefly jadeite. The Imperial Jade of charming pale or apple-green color, known as Feitsui and set down by some writers as chrysoprase, is more properly prehnite. The nephrite charms—Piedras Hijadas—known in Mexico as Chalchihuith when the Spanish invaded that country were probably jadeites.

The Chinese have held the jade family in the highest esteem and reverence for many centuries, and it poetically expresses to them all the virtues of many precious stones blended together. It is said that most of the nephrite used by them came from the Kuen-lun mountains in Turkestan, but the discovery of the mineral at no great distance from Peking in 1891 helped to make that city a great working center. The Chinese word for jade is Yu, expressed in their hieroglyph as a cross over a kind of semi-circle. Jade stone they know as Yu-chi, and precious objects of jade as Ouan Yu. The words Khitchinjou-yu indicates a gem rare as jade, and the Imperial Academy was known as Jade Hall. The Turkestan name for jade closely resembles the Chinese Yu in its form Yashm, Yushm, or Yeshm.

Ages before the Christian era, jade was said to indicate the nine accomplishments—Charity, Goodness, Virtue, Knowledge, Skill, Morality, Divination, Rectitude, and Harmony. Yu may also be rendered "courage," and in its connection with the jade stone or Yu-chi it included the five cardinal virtues—Yu, bravery; Jiu, charity; Ji, modesty; Ketsu, equity; Chi, discrimination. In her *Wanderings in China* , Mrs. C. F. Gordon Cummings says, "The Chinese name for jade is Yu-shek (it may also be written Yu-chi) and that by which we call it is said to be a corruption of a Spanish word referring to a superstition of the Mexican Indians who deemed that to wear a bracelet of this stone was the surest protection against all diseases of the loins: hence the Spanish named the mineral piedra di hijada (stone of the loins) by which name it became known in Europe."

Jade is the concentrated element of love which protected the infant and the adult and preserved the bodies of the dead from decay. Dr. Kunz quotes the Chinese mystical writer Ko Kei who asserted that the body of a man who had consumed five pounds weight of jade powdered did not change color when he died, and that when several years later he was exhumed, no evidences of change or decay were visible.

When vibrated this stone produces musical notes, and it was regarded as expressive of music and harmony, poets singing its praises. It was the emblem of love, beauty, protection, and charm, and it graced the holy altars. For the altar of earth the symbolic jade stone was of a yellowish hue, while during lunar festivals white jade was employed. Black—mentioned, but doubtful indeed—was the North Jade, and red the South. White was the West and green the East. It was said that in sickness the heat of the body drew out virtues from the jade, healing virtues soothing and life protecting.

In *Buddhist Records of the Western World*, Mr. Samuel Beal writes that "in the kingdom of Kuichi or Kuche in the Eastern Convent known as the Buddha Pavilion, there is a large yellowish-white jade stone shaped like a sea shell which bears on its surface what is said to be Buddha's footmark. This footmark is one foot eight inches long and eight inches in breadth. It is said that the relic emits a bright sparkling light at the conclusion of each fast day." Professor E. H. Parkes, M. A. in *Ancient China Simplified* mentions a custom of burying a jade symbol of rulership in the ancestral temple to protect the fortunes of the family, and jade symbols adorned private family insignia.

Strangely enough, the world's people have always revered the nephrite as the kidney stone. The use of it goes further back than the knowledge of man. It was used in old Egypt as in old China, and Pliny mentions the Adadu-nephros or kidney of Adonis. This is an early identification of jade with the Venusian Adonis and the parts of the body over which Venus astrologically presides. The Indians call it the Divine Stone which is credited with being a cure for gravel and epilepsy and as a charm against the bites of animals and poisonous reptiles. It was also said to remove thirst and hunger, to cure heartburn and asthma, and to affect favorably the voice, organs of the throat, the liver, and the blood. Its greasy surface led to its employment as a hair improver, but its chief excellence was in nephritic disorders, and specimens worn over the region of the kidneys or on the arm are said to have acted in a wonderful and unexpected manner in the banishing of these troubles. It is claimed also as a power for the removal of gravel.

The Maoris of New Zealand, according to the best authorities, noted six varieties of jade. Punamu is their name for the whole species termed by authors of the last decade "green tale of the Maoris." The well-known greenstone variety is termed Kawakawa by the Maoris, the paler and more precious Kahurangi, the grayish Inanga. The Tangiwai stone is a pellucid serpentine or variety of bowenite. The nephrite is a sacred stone to these sturdy New Zealanders, who use it in the construction of their offensive and defensive weapons and sacred objects. These greenstone weapons are amongst the finest of known stone tools. The sacred and curiously formed charm, the Hei Tiki, is an esoteric symbol which is worn as a precious emblem and never parted with except for very weighty reasons. For example, a Hei Tiki recently handled by the author was given by an old chief on his deathbed to an English officer who had saved his life in the Maori war. A Tahunga stone was the stone of the magicians by the aid of which the flashes of light were directed by the medicine man to bewildered eyes. It was usually formed from a Kahurangi type of greenstone, and the Mere or Pattoo Pattoo, a club of dark Punamu, was said to send its victims to the world of spirits.

A variety of jade of dark green color, discovered in the Swiss lake dwellings and the dolmens of France usually in the form of Celts, was termed chloromelanite by Professor Damour. This nephrite has also been discovered in New Guinea, where it was fashioned by the natives into clubs and other implements. Other nephrites have been termed fibrolite or sillimanite. The Pate de Riz is merely a fine white glass, and pink jade is usually a piece of quartz. Some beautiful specimens of translucent green jade are collected by children on the island of Iona, and many specimens have been unearthed in various parts of Europe. Professor Max Muller discovered in old Egypt a remarkable green stone used as a charm against hysteria. This interesting specimen is now in the Museum of Natural History, New York. The nephrite family is under the celestial Libra.

Marcasite

CHAPTER IV

OBSIDIAN-ONYX

Obsidian, a Natural Volcanic Glass: Ancient Egyptian Customs: Mexican Itztli: Statues in Obsidian: Used by Greeks and Romans: "Obsidians": "Obsidian Bomb": Bottle Stone: Mr. R. H. Walcott and His Term Obsidianites: Australites: Billitonites: Mr. F. Chapman's Theory: Superstitions of the Natives: Olivine: Derivation: Legend of the Sleeping Venus: The Gates: The Onyx Stones of the High Priest: Life and Earth Death: Antique Belief Noted by Mr. Phillips and Its Meaning: Rabbi Benoni and the Master Ragiel: Eye Stones: A Charm of Beauty: Castor at the Tomb of Aphareus: Nicolo the Aegyptilla of the Ancients: Gibraltar Stone: The Mantuan Vase: El Jaza or Stone of Sadness: Five Types of Onyx: An Onyx Staircase: Symbolical Meaning of the Strata: As Rosicrucian Stones: The Sainte Chapelle or Grand Camahieu Known as the "Apotheosis of Augustus": Peiresc Corrects a False Belief: The Carpegna Cameo: The Coronation Cameo of Augustus: True Meaning and Derivation of the Word Cameo.

OBSIDIAN:

> "There may be ranged among the kinds of glasses those which
> they call obsidiana for that they carry some resemblance of that
> stone which one Obsidius found in Aethyopia."
>
> Holland's Pliny

This natural volcanic glass obtains its name, according to Pliny, from Obsidius or, as he is sometimes called, Obsius, who discovered it in Ethiopia. It is very hard, brittle, and remarkably vitreous, and is variously colored black, pink, green, gray, striped, and spotted. It was early discovered to be a useful material from which to fashion knives, mirrors, and other objects of ornament and use. An ancient Egyptian custom of cutting the dead bodies of kings and priests with knives of obsidian was followed by the Guanchos of the Canary Islands. The ancient Mexicans used Itztli as they called it very generally in the manufacture of various implements. They quarried it from the Cerro de les Navajas, or Hill of the Knives, not far from Timapau. Pliny, noting that genuine gem stones could not be cut or scratched with obsidian, recommended the use of splinters of the substance for testing purposes. The same author, attesting the report that statues were made of obsidian, says, "I myself have seen solid statues in the material of the late Emperor Augustus of very considerable thickness." The Greeks and Romans found it an easy material for fashioning into cameos and intaglios which later were copied in glass. In the 18th century, connoisseurs applied the term "obsidians" to all antique pastes.

The so-called "Obsidian Bomb" has been much discussed and written about. Professor F. W. Rudley says, "It was believed for a long time to be a variety of obsidian but its different fusibility and its chemical composition are rather against its volcanic origin." It is known as moldavite, so-called by Mr. A. Dufrenoy from Moldanthein in Bohemia, where quantities have been found. On account of its olive-like or bottle-green color it is also called bottle stone or bouteillenstein. Dr. F. G. Suess suggested tectite from the Greek tektos, melted. Mr. R. H. Walcott called them obsidianites. They have also been termed australites, and billitonites (from Billiton Island). They were highly regarded by the Australian aboriginal as charm stones in sickness and trouble. Mr. W. F. Chapman, A.L.S., of the Melbourne Museum, agrees with Professor Rutley as to the non-volcanic origin of the obsidianite, and indicates the action of lightning in their formation. In this he would have the support of the ancient student who connected obsidian with the heavenly Aquarius, the "sign of the air."

OLIVINE: So-called by Werner in 1790 (see Chrysolite)

ONYX:

> "Called by the onyx round the sleeper stand
> Black dreams; and phantoms rise, a grisly band."
> Marbodus

The onyx derives its name from the Greek onyx, Onychos, a fingernail, and is a variety of chalcedony. It has been variously written as onyx stone, onyx, onix, oniche, onice, and onyse. The name of the stone is said to have sprung from the legend which tells that Cupid, finding Venus asleep on the river bank, cut her nails with the sharp point of his arrow. In this story is enwrapped the mystery of earth birth which through love enters the gate of Cancer and, with the aid of the moistures, materializes. The same parallel is expressed in the Book of Genesis, where it is written that previous to the birth of the world the "Spirit of God moved upon the face of the waters." This occult philosophy is stressed by the Platonist Macrobius who writes that the soul descending to the sphere of its spiritual death, the earth, passes through Cancer, the Gate of Man, and enters under planetary conditions that influence earth matters. On the way, it receives the souls of the planets to whose influence it is exposed while manifesting in an earth body. As the soul descends it gathers sensations and earthy feelings from the celestial Leo, and long before its absolutely material birth, obtains its first breath of matter.

Herein is the mystery of the "two onyx stones enclosed in mountings of gold graven with the names of the twelve tribes of Israel which he put on the shoulders of the ephod that they should be stones for a memorial to the children of Israel, as the Lord commanded Moses." As previously noted, on one onyx the names of six tribes were engraved, on the other the names of the remaining six, and each tribe was symbolized by a sign of the zodiac. The two onyx stones are the material emblems of the two Gates—the Gate of Cancer and the Gate of Capricorn—through which the self or soul enters and leaves the earth sphere, gathering first and throwing off afterwards the earth elements from ethereal to gross, from gross to ethereal, as described by Macrobius.

Many of the writers of the Middle Ages place the onyx under the signs Cancer and Capricorn, and there is no reason to oppose them. The onyx of Cancer is white and light-colored, while that of Capricorn, is black. The birth of the child is white and bright; with black and somber colors, those on earth mourn for the earth loss of the departed. So the "coming in" and the "going out" symbolized by the two stones of onyx set in gold, the metal of the Sun, in true talismanic style, was the memorial to the children of Israel, as it is to the world's children forever.

Phillips, an author of the middle 17th century, notes an old belief that onyx is the congealed juice of a tree called Onycha, which is commanded to be used in a sacred way in the 34th verse of the 30th chapter of Exodus, and which Emanuel Swedenborg corresponds to "interior natural truth." The statement, then, that onyx is the congealed juice of the onycha is but a cryptic way of expressing the congealing of the waters of generation—a method followed by the occult masters through the ages. Old Rabbi Benoni sees in the onyx a bound spirit which, wakeful by night only, disturbs the wearer in sleep. The master Ragiel in his *Book of Wings* recommends that a camel's head or the heads of two goats among myrtles be cut on an onyx to control and constrain demons and to make the wearer see the terrors of the night during sleeping hours. This refers to the dark of saturnine onyx which is also recommended to be enclosed in a setting of lead (metal of Saturn) and engraved with the figure of a king crowned or a

witch seated on a dragon, especially in the practice of dark or doubtful occult things.

Certain varieties of onyx presenting the appearance of an eye were
largely employed as eye stones, and it was recommended that such specimens be lightly rubbed over the closed eyelids after work wherein the eyes
have been employed. Leonardus, of the 16th century, says that this onyx
enters the eye of its own accord, and if it find anything within that is nox-
ious, it drives it out and tempers the hurtful and contrary humors. As a
higher saturnine stone, the onyx aids spiritual inspirations and helps the
wearer to restrain excessive passion. In the writer's book *Zodiacal Symbology and Its Planetary Power*, the first degree of the sign Cancer is symbolized as "a curious ring set with a large heart of white onyx." The 1st,
2nd, 10th, 11th, 12th, 28th, and 29th degrees of Cancer are much influ-
enced by the planet Venus, and to these degrees especially applied the
white onyx engraved with a figure of Venus, a charm recommended by old
masters as a talisman of beauty and strength. It was considered ideal for a
baby girl born under those degrees of Cancer according to astrophilosophy. Mr. King mentions a beautifully executed onyx intaglio showing
Castor naked, in his hand a large broadsword, weeping over the tomb of
Aphareus. The onyx in this case would be of a more somber hue and
would be classed amongst the saturnine or mourning varieties.

The famous Nicolo—known as Aegyptilla by the ancient Romans—
was obtained by cutting a blue section surrounded by black out of the
stone which then presented a fine turquoise blue with a deep black base.
On this stone some of the finest ancient work is found. It is supposed to
have obtained its name from the Greek word Nikolaus: "It is a strange
derivation," wrote Mr. King, "from the Greek was to suit the virtue ascribed to it, as if it meant Victor of Nations." Its modern derivation is from
onicolo, an Italian word signifying a little onyx. A variety of onyx marble
with bands of brown, found in the cavern limestone of Gibraltar, is known
as Gibraltar Stone. Professor Dana mentions the famous Mantuan vase at
Brunswick which, cut from a single stone 7 by 2 1/2 inches, takes the
form of a cream pot. The color is brown, and its raised figures of white
and yellow, illustrate Ceres and Triptolemus searching for the lost Proser-
pine. The Saturn side of the onyx is taken by the Arabs, who call it el jaza
or sadness, but the color was always considered and the varieties were
thus identified:

1. Those resembling the human fingernail, under Cancer.
2. White striped with red, under Cancer.
3. White striped with black, under Capricorn.
4. Black, unstriped, under Capricorn (probably the true El Jaza).
5. Black with white stripes, under Capricorn.

One of the most remarkable pieces of modern work in onyx is said to be the staircase of a New York millionaire. The cost of this is set down as $300,000.

The sardonyx or sardian onyx, as it is sometimes called, was written at various periods as sardonyse, sardony, sardonix, sardonice, sardonyches, sarderyk, sardonique, and sardonick. Swedenborg corresponds it to love of good and light. It exhibits sard and white chalcedony in layers. Some ancient authors account as fine only those specimens which exhibit three layers at least: a black base, a white zone, and a layer of red or brown—the black symbolizing humility, the white virtue, and the red fearlessness. The sardonyx is under the heavenly Leo, the sign of sensation, feeling, "the first aspect of its (the soul's) future condition here below."

In the Rosicrucian jewels, the sardonyx appears as the gem of victorious ecstasy and rapture which flow from the eternal font of delight, banishing grief and woe. It was said to give self-control, conjugal happiness, and good fortune. It is also said that if the woman whose talismanic stone it is neglects to wear it she will never marry. It was frequently engraved with an eagle or a hawk as a talisman of fortune. It is under the celestial Leo.

The "Sainte Chapelle," the second largest cameo known, is stated by Sir William Smith and others to measure 12 x 10 1/2 inches. Mr. C. W. King gives the measurements as about 13 x 11 inches and states that it is a sardonyx of five layers. The central carving of this "Grand Camahieu," as it was called, represents the return of Germanicus from Germany in the year 17 A.D., Tiberius and Livia enthroned receiving him. In exergue, the grief-stricken captives are shown. Above is the apotheosis of Augustus by which the whole work is now known. This remarkable cameo was for a long time believed to typify "the triumph of Joseph in Egypt," and was regarded as a sacred relic. The learned Nicholas Claude Fabri de Peiresc, the great antiquary of France, proved in 1619 the falsity of this inconceivable belief, and was the first to classify correctly the subject of this massive gem. By pawning this sardonyx to Louis X of France for 10,000 silver marks, the unfortunate Baldwin II, Emperor of Constantinople, was able to save his throne a little longer. This cameo is in the Bibliotheque Nationale, Paris.

Another five strata sardonyx cameo—the largest known—is the Carpegna cameo, formerly in the possession of Cardinal Carpegna and now in the Vatican. This large specimen is 16 by 12 inches. "The subject," writes Mr. King, "is the Pompa di Bacco, or Bacchus and Ceres," Virgil's "duo clarissima mundi lumina," as symbolizing the Sun and Moon, standing upon a magnificent car, the god holding a vase a thyrsus, the goddess her bunch of wheat ears. On his right stands winged Comus. The car is drawn by four centaurs, two male and two female. The first male bears a rhyton and a thyrsus, the second a torch while he snaps the fingers of his right hand. One female centaur plays the double flute, the other a tambourine. On the ground lie the mystic basket and two huge vases. The large cameo, 9 by 8 inches, known as the "Coronation of Augustus," shows that Emperor enthroned, holding a sceptre in his right hand with Livia by his side as Roma. Between Augustus and Livia is the zodiacal sign Capricorn, under the third degree of which Augustus was born, according to Firmicus. Beneath the various figures (Neptune, Cybele, Drusus, Tiberius, Victory, Antonia, wife of Drusus as Abundantia, and her children Germanicus and Claudius), are Roman soldiers erecting trophies, their unhappy captives in the foreground.

The word "cameo" is said to be of unknown derivation. Dr. Brewer says it means "onyx" and there seems evidence enough to indicate that on account of the great use of onyx and sardonyx for cutting symbolic figures in relief, the term onyx was usually accepted as indicating the completed work. The derivation from the Arabic chemeia, a charm, is noted by Mr. King who draws attention to the light in which such relics were universally considered in those ages, by Orientals and Europeans alike. The Arabic word has affinity with the Talmudical Hebrew word khemeia, an amulet; and there seems little reason to doubt that chemeia or khemeia is the parent of our word "cameo," known in the ancient world as an onyx, meaning a charm, an amulet, or a talisman.

CHAPTER V

THE OPAL

The Opal in Astrophilosophy: Petrus Arlensis Describes the Opal: Pliny's Poetical Opinion: The Paederos Child Beautiful as Love: The Orphan: Roman Senator and His Opal: Ophthalmios the Eye Stone: Opinion of Medieval Writers: The Bay Tree: Albertus Magnus and the Opals that Sparkled in Darkness: The Zodiacal Sign of Royalty and the Opal: Keraunios or the Thunder Stone: The Beauty Stone: The Stone of Hope, Achievement and Love: The Large Hungarian Opal: Australian Opal Fields: Sir David Brewster's Theory of Colors in Opal: Dr. G. F. H. Smith's Explanation: Sensitiveness of the Opal: Superstition Against Opal: The Plague at Venice: The "Burning of Troy": The Crimean War: Scott's Anne of Geierstein: Combinations of Diamonds and Opals: Destruction of the Vanities at Florence: Story of the Opal of Alfonzo XII of Spain: A Cholera Stone Fatal to the King and to All Who Received It from Him According to Astrological Science: The Baron's Opal of Fortune.

OPAL:

"Everyone knows how capriciously the colours of a fine opal vary from day to day and how rare the lights are which fully bring them out."

Ruskin

The word "opal" is derived from the Latin opalus, and is identified with the Sanskrit upala, a precious stone. It appears under the forms opale, opall, opalle, opalis, and ophal.

This beautiful inimitable gem is a hydrous silica and is allied to the non-metallic minerals of the agate family from which, however, it differs in brilliancy, luster, and degree of hardness. It is sensitive to the action of strong chemicals and does not present, like other minerals, crystalline form. As a gem of the Sun, it exhibits flows of fire like the Sun at midsummer, as a gem of Venus, its delicate beauty radiates her colorful charms; and as a gem of Uranus, its refusal to submit to the all-embracing law of mineral structure harmonizes with the iconoclastic character of that planet according to astrophilosophy.

Ancient and modern poets unite in singing the praises of the opal. Over 2,400 years ago, Onomacritus, known as the religious poet of the ancient Greeks, wrote that "the delicate colour and tenderness of the opal reminded him of a loving and beautiful child." Joshua Sylvester (16th century) wrote of "the opal-coloured morn," and the poet Campbell of a time when "the opal morn just flushed the sky," thus echoing William Drummond of Hawthornden's:

> "Aurora. . .with her opal light
> Night's horrours checketh, putting stars to flight."

Emerson wrote of the "opal-coloured days," and Poe with true poetic fancy saw even the air opal tinted:

> "A wreath that twined each starry form around
> And all the opal'd air in colour bound."

Shakespeare, in *Twelfth Night,* links the mind of the Duke with the opal (written "opall" in early editions). Boetius, Cardanus, and a host of writers pay their tributes to the "orphan" of the Greeks, and Petrus Arlensis wrote, "The various colours in the opal tend greatly to the delectation of the sight; nay, more, they have the greatest efficacy in cheering the heart, and the inward parts especially rejoice the eyes of the beholders. One in particular came into my hands in which such beauty, loveliness, and grace shone forth that it could truly boast that it forcibly drew all other gems to itself, while it surprised, astonished and held captive without escape or intermission the hearts of all who beheld it. It was of the size of a filbert and clasped in the claws of a golden eagle wrought with wonderful art; and had such vivid and various colors that all the beauties of the heavens might be viewed within it. Grace went out from it, majesty shot forth from its almost divine splendor. It sent forth such bright and piercing rays that it struck terror into all beholders. In a word it bestowed upon the wearer the qualities granted by Nature to itself, for by an invisible dart it penetrated the souls and dazzled the eyes of all who saw it: appalled the hearts, however bold and courageous: in fine, it filled with trembling the bodies of the bystanders and forced them by a fatal impulse to love, honor and worship it. I have seen, I have felt, I call God to witness: of a truth such a stone is to be valued at an inestimable amount."

Turning back again, we read Pliny's poetical opinion that "the opal is made up of the glories of the most precious gems which make description so difficult. For amongst them is the gentler fire of the ruby, the rich purple of the amethyst, the sea-green of the emerald, glittering together in union indescribable. Others by the intensity of their hues equal all the painter's colours, others the flame of burning brimstone or of fire quickened by oil." In admiration, the Romans called the gem Cupid-Paederos, child beautiful as love; and it was also known as Orphanus, the orphan, because of its isolated glory. Leonardus wrote that it partook of all the virtues of those stones whose colors it showed, and Porta said that it not only drove away despondency but malignant affections also. So highly valued was the stone in the ancient world that the Roman Senator Nonius, who wore an opal ring worth 20,000 sesterces, preferred to be exiled rather than give it up when Marcus Antonius wished to purchase it to present to the Egyptian Queen Cleopatra. This famous ring was discovered some few years back in the tomb of the firm-willed senator of old Rome.

Opal was called opthalmios or eye stone in the Middle Ages, and in the time of Queen Elizabeth it was written ophal and opall. In *Rare* Ben Jonson writes of an opal "wrapped in a bay leaf in my left fist to charm their eyes with." The opal—ophthalmis lapis—was famous as an eyestone, taking precedence over the emerald and all gems credited with such virtue. It was advised by medieval writers that it be wrapped in a bay leaf to sharpen the sight of the owner and to blunt that of others with whom he came in contact, hence also its reputed virtue of bestowing the gift of invisibility, which earned it the name "Patronus furum," the patron of thieves.

The bay tree is identified in astrophilosophy as a tree of the Sun and the zodiacal Leo (House of the Sun), and is an ancient charm against evil forces, thunder, lightning, and the afflictions of Saturn, the heavenly symbol of light. Albertus Magnus, regarding the opal as a symbol of the loveliness of light, says that "at one time, but not in our age, it sparkled in the dark." The zodiacal Leo or Lion is the ancient sign of royalty, and old writers say that kingly government was established on the earth in the Leonine age. Alluding to the great translucent opal in the Crown of the Holy Roman Empire, Albertus said that it safeguarded the honor of the kings.

The stone was always considered to protect the wearer from cholera, kidney troubles, and similar diseases; to soothe the heart, the eyes, and the nerves; and to protect from the lightning stroke. The belief in its power to ward off lightning was universal in the ancient world, when amongst the people it was believed to have fallen from the heavens during thunderstorms—hence its old name, keraunios, thunder stone, amongst the

Greeks and ceraunium amongst the Romans. The opal was essentially the stone of beauty, which coveted gift it bestowed upon the wearer who, however, must have entered earth life with the Sun in Leo (approximately between July 24th and August 24th), Libra (September 24th to October 24th), or Aquarius (January 21st to February 19th). It favored children, the theater, amusements, friendships, and the feelings. Held between the eyes, it gave proper direction to thoughts. Held in the left hand and gazed upon, it favored desires. It is the stone of hope and achievement and has been truly described as the "gem of the gods." Above all, it is a stone of love. But if the lover be false, its influence is reversed, and opal proves a sorry gem for faithless lovers. Mr. Emanuel comments on the two fine opals which were amongst the imperial jewels of France, one of which was set in the clasp of the royal cloak. The opal, astrologically considered, is one of the fortunate gems for France.

A beautiful uncut opal, discovered at Czernovitza in Hungary, has been valued at over 50,000 pounds sterling. This specimen, 5 by 2 1/2 inches and weighing 3,000 carats, was placed in the Museum of Natural History at Vienna. The mines at Czernovitza are known to have been worked over 500 years ago, and at a more remote period, they no doubt supplied the ancient world. There is little doubt, however, that the wonderful opals from Australia's fields have eclipsed anything yet found. The White Cliffs, the Lightning Ridge, and the newer field in the Northwest are responsible for some of the most beautiful gems that have ever been unearthed. A kangaroo hunter accidentally discovered the White Cliffs field in New South Wales over 40 years ago. Rich "blacks" were discovered later in the iron sandstone of Lightning Ridge (New South Wales), and the new fields northwest of Tarcoola are yielding white and light varieties. Opal country is dry and dreary, and the diggers deserve all they find.

Sir David Brewster's theory of the color blends which flash from an opal is that

> "the stone is internally traversed with undulating fissures of microscopic minuteness upon which refraction and decomposition of light takes place. The variations in the nature of these minute cavities cause the appearance of the opal to vary considerably, and the different effects of colour thus produced are technically known as the pattern of the gem."

Hauy held that color in the opal is caused by thin films of air which fill the interior cavities. Dr. G. F. Herbert Smith writes that "the colouration is not due to ordinary absorption but to the action of cracks in the stone.

This is shown by the fact that the transmitted light is complementary to the reflected light; the blue opal, for instance, is a yellow when held up so that light has passed through it. . . ."

"Opal differs," he says, "from the rest of the principal gem stones in being not a crystalline body but a solidified jelly, and it depends for its attractiveness upon the characteristic play of colour known, in consequence, as opalescence which arises from a peculiarity in the structure. Opal is mainly silica (Si O2) in composition, but it contains in addition an amount of water, thereby differing slightly in refractivity from the original substance. The structure not being quite homogeneous, each crack has the same action upon light as a soap-film and gives rise to precisely similar phenomena: the thinner and more uniform the cracks, the greater the splendour of the chromatic display, the particular tint depending upon the direction in which the stone is viewed. The cracks in certain opals are not filled up, and therefore contain air." The opal is a very sensitive gem and should not be put near strong acids nor greasy substances. The heat of the body improves its luster for the opal is essentially a stone to be worn, but it is unsafe to put these gems near liquids or to submit them to fire.

"Truth is as impossible to be soiled by any outward touch as the sunbeam."

Milton

Perhaps against no other gem has the bigotry of superstitious ignorance so prevailed as against the wonderful opal. The reason for it apparently dates no further back than the 14th century. It was at this time that the dreaded Black Death was carrying off thousands of people in Europe. The year 1348, an astrological martial subcycle, saw Venice assailed by destructive earthquakes, tidal waves, and the plague.   In a few months, the epidemic carried off two-fifths of the population of the city, sparing neither rich nor poor, young nor old. It is said that at this time the opal was a favorite gem with Italian jewelers, being much used in their work. It is further said that opals worn by those stricken became suddenly brilliant and that the luster entirely departed with the death of the wearer. Story further tells that the opal then became an object of dread and was associated with the death of the victim. On the astrological side, it might be considered that the city of Venice comes under the watery Cancer, and cannot, therefore, claim the opal as its jewel. But admitting that under special and rare conditions certain diseases can influence the opal if worn on the body, the truth of the Venice story can be reasonably doubted.

Another theory of the origin of the superstition is traced to the rigorous order of Jerome Savonarola for the destruction of the vanities in the year

1497. This remarkable ascetic caused great bonfires to be lighted in various parts of the city of Florence, the largest in the Piazza Signoria. Into these bonfires were thrown works of art and beauty, pictures, statues, jewels, and beautiful raiment. The fanatical spirit so gained ground owing to the impassioned preaching of Savonarola that women threw into the flames their costliest jewels, authors their books, students their manscripts, and poets their love songs. It is assumed that the opal, the gem and symbol of the beauties of Venus, came under the ban; and history relates that the most direct onslaughts were made on the pictures and statues of the goddess. Astrologers show that the year 1497 was dominated by the planet of war and destruction, Mars; and it is deplorable that so many wonderful works were sacrificed during that unhappy period. The artist F. W. W. Topham, R.I., has illustrated this event in his well-known painting, "Renouncing the Vanities by Order of Savonarola," which picture now hangs in the Art Gallery of New South Wales.

There is also a story which tells that during the Crimean War the gem was popular with the English army and navy and that it was found in quantities on the bodies of the slain. Sir Walter Scott's romantic story, *Anne of Geierstein*, was a powerful influence in advancing the superstition against the opal, although Sir Walter alluded to the Mexican Opal known as Girasol and not to the better known precious opal. Even while these superstitions were growing, to dream of an opal was regarded as an indication of great possessions, of the favor of ladies and people of influence, and—if the stone be dark—of sudden happenings of a beneficial nature.

Another modern superstition says that it is not fortunate to set opals and diamonds together in jewels. Quabalistically, opals and diamonds are set down as particularly harmonious stones which, in combination, have a fortunate and positive-negative influence. Astrologically, the diamond is attached to the zodiacal signs Aries, Leo, and Libra, and the opal to Leo, Libra, and Aquarius, and astrology is absolutely the special guide to talismanic construction. The fine fiery opal known as the "Burning of Troy" was given by Napoleon to Josephine and is sometimes quoted as evidence of the evil power of opals. It rather provides peculiar testimony in favor of old talismanic lore. This opal was lost and has never since been found—opals would be regarded as unfavorable for Josephine.

Passing over trivial superstitions containing neither truth nor interest, we may conclude this section with the story of the Grand Opal of Spain, which is said to have brought disaster to the Royal House.

When Alfonzo XII of Spain was a wanderer, he was deeply attracted by and fell in love with the Comtesse de Castiglione, then a reigning beauty. Immediately after Alfonzo became King, the Comtesse hastened to greet him with the fond desire to become his queen. However, when she found that he had set her aside and married the Princess Mercedes, her anger knew no bounds. Resolving on revenge, she sent Alfonzo "in memory of the old friendship" a wedding present of a magnificent opal set in a filagree ring of gold—a style of mounting in great favor with the jewelers of Spain.

The delicacy of the jewel so attracted Queen Mercedes that she asked

HOROSCOPE OF   ALFONZO XII

Astrologically the opal would be accounted unfortunate for this King

the King to grace her finger with it. A few months afterwards, she died of a mysterious illness, and Alfonzo gave the ring so admired by her to Queen Christina, his grandmother, whose death shortly followed. The King then presented the ring to his sister, the Infanta Maria del Pilar, who was in turn carried off by the same mysterious illness. A few weeks afterwards, the King's sister-in-law, the youngest daughter of the Duc and

Duchesse de Montpensier, who had asked the King for the ring, also died. The King then placed it on his own finger, and in a little time, the same illness which had affected his wife and kindred ended his troubled earth life. After these calamities Queen Christina attached the ring to a chain of gold and set it about the neck of the patron saint of Madrid, the Virgin of Alumdena.

Ancient philosophy would have depreciated the wearing or giving of an opal by Alfonzo XII of Spain. At this time, it must be remembered, cholera was raging throughout Spain, over 100,000 people died of it during the summer and autumn of 1885. It attacked all classes from the palace of the King to the hut of the peasant, some accounts giving the death estimate at 50 percent of the population. It would be as obviously ridiculous to hold the opal responsible for this scourge as it was to do so in the case of the previously noted plague at Venice. All that may be said is that, in this case, the opal was not a talisman for good for King Alfonzo XII of Spain and to those who received it from his hand, and that in the philosophy of sympathetic attraction and apathetic repulsion man, stones, metals, and all natural objects come under the same law. We may wonder why the King gave this opal from one of his relatives to another, but the reputation of the opal as a charm against cholera (noted in the previous chapter) must have reached the King. In the intensity of his worry, he used a charm, which according to the ancients, would act in his hands fatally instead of beneficially.

In the month of October 1908, a French baron, sitting in the stalls of the London Pavilion during Mr. and Mrs. Marriott's thought-reading exhibition, handed an opal of uncommon form to Mr. Marriott. Mrs. Marriott seated on the stage with bandaged eyes gave an accurate description of it, saying further that it was a stone of fortune to the owner who was about to become the possessor of over half a million pounds. The Baron, who had resided in London for 18 years, was interviewed by a representative of the *Evening News* on the following day. He communicated the fact that a few days before, he had, through the death of a relative in Mexico, become heir to property worth over 500,000 pounds, yielding an income of 25,000 pounds per annum. The Baron who cherished the opal as his sympathetic luck stone, told the newspaperman that:

"It is an uncut stone which has been in the possession of my family since the twelfth century. We have always had the tradition that it will bring good fortune to any direct descendant of the family in the male line who holds it.

"A curious stipulation, however, of the tradition is that the person who has it must possess qualities which have a sympathetic attraction to the stone in order that its beneficent effect may be felt. On a flat surface of the opal is a word in old Spanish, now only dimly seen, which means in English 'good luck.'

"I have treasured the gem as an heirloom, but have thought little of the tradition until lately, when a member of the cadet branch of the family died and left me the immense fortune I have mentioned to you. I can hardly realize all that it means to me as yet. Up to now my income has not been much more than 500 pounds, and to suddenly find 25,000 pounds a year at one's disposal is a little staggering.

"There have been one or two previous instances where my ancestors while holding the opal have experienced exceptionally good luck, but, personally, I have not ever paid much regard to the old tradition. You may imagine, however, that the gem will be most carefully preserved by me."

CHAPTER VI

THE GREAT AUSTRALIAN OPAL
THE FLAME QUEEN

"But who can paint
Like Nature? Can imagination boast
Amid its gay creation hues like hers?"
Thomson

The Flame Queen, the rarest opal yet won from the barren sun-baked fields of Lightning Ridge, New South Wales, near the borders of Queensland, Australia, takes its place amongst the famous gems of the world.

It is a large oval-shaped stone measuring 2.8 inches by 2.3 inches and weighing 253 carats. In structure and color it is unique, the center slightly in relief while the surrounding border stands out boldly as a frame to a picture. When one looks directly at the stone, the inspiration of the name becomes manifest. The center, a deep flame, burns scarlet; and two slight depressions almost parallel to each other give the impression of erupting fire mountains, the lower of which flings two triangular shafts towards the enclosing green frame. Viewed from another angle, the burning center yields as if by magic to a field of cool yet vivid emerald, and the frame to a royal blue. Another angle shows a bronze center touched with points of darker hue within a frame of changing blue and amethyst. The stone is chameleon-like, bewildering in its living beauty.

This stone is the choicest gem in the Kelsey I. Newman collection of rare opals and precious stones. On the 6th of March, 1916, Mr. Allan Harris of Brisbane submitted the gem to the Queensland Geological Survey. In the course of his report, Mr. B. Dunstan, the chief Government Geologist, mentioned that the back of the stone "is impressed with what appears to be a fossil plant called Ginko, which occurs in the Jurassic rocks of Queensland but not in association with any opal deposits. The stone is a wonderful specimen and much the largest gem of its class that has ever come under my notice." This beautiful opal, unlike some other famous gems mentioned in this book, is said to have brought good fortune to all who have been associated with it.

CHAPTER VII

VARIOUS KINDS OF OPAL

"Grey years ago a man lived in the east,
Who did possess a ring of worth immense,
From a beloved hand. Opal the stone,
Which flashed a hundred bright and beauteous hues,
And had the secret power to make beloved
Of God and man the blessed and fortunate
Who wore it in this faith and confidence."
Nathan the Wise, Lessing

CACHOLONG: An opaque white or bluish-white variety of opal which obtains its name from the river Cach in Bokhara, according to some authorities, and from the Tartars, according to others. The Easterners set a high value on the stone which glistens with the opalescent gleam of Mother of Pearl. It is associated with chalcedony and being of a porous nature sticks to the tongue when touched by it. The cacholong is a stone of pure friendship, sincerity, and truth.

FLOAT STONE: A porous opal of a fibrous type which floats on water. It occurs in concretionary masses and is esteemed as a stone over which the most sacred promises may be made. Lovers join hands over a float stone floating in a vessel of water and pledge their troth with the utmost solemnity, misfortune being bound to dog the footsteps of the faithless one.

GIRASOL: The girasol is the Mexican fire opal which reflects hyacinth and yellow colors. Good specimens are attractive and fairly popular. This is the opal indicated in Scott's *Anne of Geierstein.*

HYALITE: The hyalite is derived from the Greek word for glass, and the stone, a transparent glass-like opal, has been called Muller's Glass by Dr. A. G. Werner who is said to have discovered it. It is very like clear gum arabic and is probably one of the esteemed eye stones of the old writers.

HYDROPHANE: This variety of opal is very porous and becomes beautifully translucent and opalescent after being left for a little time in water. It is otherwise of an opaque white or yellow and not very attractive. In the United States it has been termed magic stone.

MENILITE: This variety is found in slate not far from the French capitol. It is also termed liver opal, and is said to have talismanic action on that organ. It is a concretionary opal, brown or liver-colored.

OPAL JASPER: Opal jasper is a jasper-like, resinous, dark red, ferruginous variety of opal. It is identified as the opal of beautiful wisdom.

ROSE OPAL: This is a beautiful rose-colored opal found at Quincy in France. Rose opal is the opal of the baby cupid and is termed the opal of childhood.

SEMI-OPAL: A silicified wood-opal of waxy luster, transparent to opaque. It is found in various colors—white, brown, grey, red, blue, and green. It has the appearance of petrified wood. It is a tree-growing charm and is no doubt the forest opal.

TABASHEER: Its name corrupted from Tabixir, this siliceous aggregation is found in the joints of certain bamboo known in the Malay as the Mali Mali, Rotan jer' nauf (blood of the dragon Rattan) and Buluh Kasap (rough bamboo). In appearance it is generally like clear gum arabic, although sometimes opaque, and is the sap transformed by evaporation. Under reflective light it is blue, and under transmitted light it is either light yellow or amber-red. It is extremely absorptive.

In Marco Polo's account of the expedition of the Great Kaan against Chipangu, we are told that "when the people of the Kaan had landed on the great Island they stormed a tower belonging to some of the islanders who refused to surrender. Resistance being overcome, the Kaan's soldiers cut off the heads of all the garrison except eight. On these eight they found it impossible to inflict any wound. Now this was by virtue of certain stones which they had in their arms inserted between the skin and the flesh with such skill as not to show at all externally. And the charm and virtue of the stones were such that those who wore them would never perish by steel.

So when the Kaan's generals heard this they ordered that the prisoners be beaten to death with clubs. After their death the stones were extracted from their bodies and were greatly prized." Friar Odoric says that these stones of invulnerability were Tabashir specimens which were used by the natives of the Indian Islands where their virtue was esteemed. According to Avicenna, the Tabashir was a powerful eye stone and remover of past fears, present dreads, and future anxieties.

PSEUDOMORPHIC OPAL: Opalized shells and bones are found in quantities in opal country. These specimens are unique and of much curious interest. A number of shells from the fields 150 miles northwest of Tarcoola (on the East-West Railway, over 250 miles fromm Port Augusta) were submitted to the author. In these the silica slowly and progressively took the place of the primary substance until it was completely opalized, retaining the old form of the material. It is remarkable to contemplate the change of conditions which placed the former substance so completely at the mercy of the consuming opal. Such transformation is continual in nature, manifesting variously in the mineral world, proving that eternal progress is eternal change. It was the observation of similar material phenomena that led ancient scientists to the conclusion that transformations could be accomplished by the skill, knowledge, and wisdom of sincere and gifted men who persevered, undaunted by superficial criticism. The triumphs of the chemist served to indicate how much more could be done by those brave enough to prove the immortality of man by reducing the unknown to terms of the known. The word pseudomorph is derived from the Greek pseudo and morphes, disguising one's form.

CHAPTER VIII

PEARL

Pearl: How Produced: Symbolic Stories of the Ancients: Boethius and the River Pearls: Vishnu Creates Pearls: Pearls in the Ramayana: Sandius's Contribution to the Royal Society of London in 1673: Sir Everard Home and Darwin on the Formation of Pearls: Mr. Kelaart's Reports to the Government of Ceylon: Researches of Professors Herdmann, Hornel and Seurat: The Time of Pearl Maturity: Home on the Luster of the Pearl: The Form of a Pearl: The Process of "Skinning": Jerome and the Story of the Doves: The Pearl of Prince Imenheit: The Great Persian Pearl: The Hope Pearl: The Austrian Imperial Pearl: La Pellegrina: The Great Southern Cross: The Pearl of Phillip II of Spain: The Pearl of the King of Maabar: The Tibetan Prayer of Victory: King Jaipal's Necklace: The Famine in Egypt: Ebu Hesham's Account of the Tomb of Princess Tajah: Benvenuto Cellini and the Pearl Necklace of the Duchess of Florence: The Pearl Rope of Marie Alexandrovna: Pink Pearls: Red Pearls: A Death Rite Mentioned By Marco Polo: Pearls Used in Buddhist Ceremonies: Julius Caesar, an Expert in Pearls: The Breastplate of Venus Genetrix: Caesar's Gift to Servilla: Pearls in the Times of the Caesars: Seneca's Cynicism: Cleopatra's Pearls: Other Pearl Swallowers: Pearls and Jewels of Mary Queen of Scotland: Pearls in Hebraic and Arabian Legend: The Pearl in China: The Pearl in Medicine: The Angel Gabriel and the Pearl: The Pearl of Paradise.

PEARL:

> "Searching the wave I won therefrom a pearl
> Moonlike and glorious, such as kings might buy
> Emptying their treasury."
>
> Arnold

The name "pearl" is derived from the Latin pilula diminutive of pila, a ball, and some of the forms of the word noted are perle, peerle, perl, perll, perill, pearel, peirle, and pearle. The pearl is a product of certain salt and fresh water shell-fish of the Aviculidae family. It is formed by the efforts of the mollusc to rid itself of irritating substances by secreting an iridescent fluid with which he lines his shell. The effect of this irritation is shown in a number of irregular tubercules inside the shell, and within these coverings is the securely protected pearl. Frequently pearls of most beautiful luster and form are found detached from the shell in the fleshy folds of the oyster, and these are said to be the most perfect. It is now quite certain that disease is not the cause, as has so generally been believed. Amongst the ancient writers, so much of the purely symbolic was set down in perfectly plain, matter-of-fact language that it is difficult to make assertions as to what was really known of the material truth. Both Pliny and Discorides poetically state that dew or rain from Heaven fell into the open pearl shells and was transformed by the secretions of the oyster into precious pearls. There is an old legend which tells that the tears of joy shed by the angels for the ultimate destiny of man were the tears that fell into the pearl oyster shell, to be transformed into beautiful pearls. Moore delightfully refers to this story:

"Precious the tear as that rain from the sky
  Which turns into pearls as it falls in the sea."

The philosopher Anicius Bothius of the 5th and 6th centuries, A.D., wrote that, when the sky is clear and the weather temperate, the fresh water pearl mussels of the Scotch rivers open their mouths just a little above water and swallow the heavenly dews, which cause the breeding of pearls. These mussels, continues the philosopher, are so sensitive that the slightest noise causes them to sink to the bottom of the river. He credits them with "knowing well in what estimation the fruit of their womb is to all people." Vishnu, according to Indian mythology, created pearls Moti by his word, and consequently these gems are foremost in the adornment of Indian deities. The *Ramayana*, perhaps the greatest poem of ancient India, narrates the story of the death of Maha Bali, telling that pearls sprung from the teeth of the slain god.

In the winter of 1673, the naturalist Sandius sent, on the authority of "Henricus Arnoldi, an ingenious Dane," a letter to the newly formed Royal Society of London:

"Pearl shells in Norway do breed in sweet waters: their shells are like mussels but larger: the fish is like an oyster producing clusters of eggs. These, when ripe, are cast out and become like those that cast them. But sometimes it appears that one or two of these eggs stick fast to the side of the matrix and are not voided with the rest. These are fed by the oyster against her will, and they do grow, according to the length of time, into pearls of different size, and do imprint a mark both on fish and shell by the situation conform to its figure."

The eminent surgeon, Sir Everard Home, unaware of the letter of Sandius, arrived at the same conclusion independently. He stated that this, "the richest jewel in a monarch's crown which cannot be imitated by any art of man, either in beauty of form or brilliancy of luster is the abortive egg of an oyster enveloped in its own nacre."

Darwin (*Economy of Vegetation*) wrote that pearls are formed "like those calcareous productions of crabs known by the name of 'crabs eyes' which are always near the stomach of the creature. In both cases the substance is probably a natural provision either for the reparation or enlargement of the shell."

Mr. Kelaart, in his reports to the Government of Ceylon (1857-1859), seems to be the first to allude to the part played by parasites in the production of pearls in tropical seas. The researches of Professors Herdman and Hornel confirmed the deductions of Kelaart that the larva of a cestoid was the identified pearl parasite. Monsieur Seurat, the French naturalist who made a long study of the pearl oyster of the Pacific, was also convinced that pearl formation was caused by a parasite. Whatever the cause of the irritability which brings into action the nacreous secretion of the tortured oyster, it is evident that the protective process is a long one. The pearl culture industry of the Chinese and Japanese has shown that it takes 12 months for the irritant to be covered with a coat of a tenth of a millimeter. A new layer is formed over the old one about once a year. Pearlers say that an oyster must be at least four years old before pearls begin to form properly, and that it takes from seven to nine years to mature.

The beautiful luster of the pearl Sir Everard Home held to arise from a central cell of bright nacre, the diaphanous substance admitting the light rays. "Upon taking a split pearl," he writes, "and putting a candle behind the cell, the surface of the pearl became immediately illuminated; and upon mounting one with coloured foil behind the cell, and by putting a candle behind the foil, the outer convex surface became universally of a beautiful pink colour." The examination of a half pearl will show the concentric formation which is like an onion, and the process called "skinning" is often resorted to in the endeavor to gain a more lustrous jewel by removing the outer layer. The translucency of the perfect pearl has not been correctly reproduced by any artificial production.

A curious passage in Jerome Cardan's *De Rerum Varietate* (16th century), repeats an old saying that the luster and polish on pearls arises from doves playing with them. To understand this seemingly absurd story, it is necessary to carry our minds far back to the famous Greek oracle at

Dodona in Epirus. According to Herodotus, the Phoenicians carried off the sacred women from Thebes in Egypt to the Libian oracle of Zeus Ammon and to Dodona; the legend at Dodona saying that they came in the form of two doves. The Greek word for "doves" is the same as that for "priestesses," namely, Peleiai. The connection can be carried further, if necessary, but it is sufficient to establish the tie between women and doves. The word *peleiai* was freely used for both and came to be employed as an endearing term for wise women. It is a proven fact and an extremely ancient one that pearls worn near the skin of a woman—especially, according to ancient philosophy, near one in whose horoscope the moon was powerfully placed at birth—are improved in luster and tone. So let the "Doves" (peleiai) be wise and play with their pearls.

Tavernier writes of "the most beautiful pearl in the world," which belonged to Imenheit, Prince of Muscat. After a lavish entertainment which the Khan of Ormus gave in honor of the prince, the latter took off a chain which he wore around his neck and to which was attached a small bag. From the bag he drew forth this wonderful pearl of perfect sphericity, so translucent that light could almost be seen through it. The weight of this gem was 12 carats, and so high a value did Prince Imenheit place on it that he refused 2,000 tomans for it from his host, who coveted it as a present for the King of Persia. He later refused an offer of 40,000 crowns by an agent of the Grand Mogul. This pearl was discovered off the Persian coast.

Another great pearl which, according to Tavernier, was the most perfect ever discovered, was found at Catifa, a famous fishery in Pliny's time. The great traveler says that the King of Persia obtained it from an Arabian merchant in 1633. It was a pearl of great size and a "pearl of great price," the king giving 1,400,000 livres (about 550,000 dollars) for it. It was pear-shaped and of perfect color and symmetry. The weight is not stated, but it was said to be about 1 1/2 inches in length and 63 inches in diameter at its greatest part.

The "Hope" pearl of cylindrical form weighs 454 carats. This gem belonged to Mr. Henry Thomas Hope, so well-known in connection with the "Hope" diamond. Another famous pearl of 300 carats once adorned the Imperial crown of Austria. "La Pellegrina," an Indian white circular pearl of 28 carats, said to be the most perfect specimen in the world today, was in the Zosima Museum, Moscow.

Nine large pearls naturally interlinked so as to form a true representation of the Southern Cross were discovered in a pearl oyster off the West Australian Coast by Mr. Kelly of Roeburn, who was familiarly known as "Shiner" Kelly. The crew of this lugger viewed it with superstitious fear, and it was buried for some years. It was afterwards resurrected and exhibited at the Colonial and Indian Exhibition, London, in 1886, where it caused some sensation. The pearls which formed the cross were at first thought by many to be joined together by craft, but experts with powerful magnifying glasses speedily dispelled this illusion and proved that nature, not man, was the artist who reproduced the Star Cross of the Heavens— the Cross of Australian Unity—in pearls in a sea oyster.

In the year 1579, a pearl of 250 carats was obtained amongst others by the agents of Philip II of Spain, from the Island of Margarita in the West Indies. It was said to be worth 150,000 dollars. Marco Polo wrote that the King of Maabar wore pearls and gems worth more than a city's ransom. "Nobody is permitted to take out of his kingdom a pearl weighing more than half a saggio (a Venetian weight, the sixth of an onze), unless he manages to do it secretly. The King every year proclaims through the realm that if anyone possesses a pearl of great worth and will bring it to him, he (the King) will pay three times as much as its value. Everybody is glad to do this and thus the King gets all into his own hands, giving every man his price." This king wore a necklace on which 104 pearls and rubies of great size were strung on fine silk, and every day, following the custom of his ancestors, he had to say 104 prayers to the gods. The number is disputed but in an occult sense the Tibetan prayer of Victory over the 104 devils seems to confirm it.

The pearl necklace which Muhammed forced the Hindu King Jaipal to surrender to him (1001 A.D.) is said to have been made of great pearls. It was valued at 20,000 dinars (more than 500,000 dollars). We read in the Book of Genesis of the terrible famine which affected the peoples of the earth and drove them to seek corn in the land of Egypt, where doubtless owing to the great pull on her stocks, some anxiety was beginning to be felt. The Arabian writer, Ebn Hesham, describes a sepulchre in Yemen which had been discovered after some heavy floods. In this sepulchre lay the embalmed body of an Arabian princess around whose neck were seven strands of pearls, age-stained and lusterless. There were rings set with precious stones on her fingers and toes, seven jeweled armlets on each of her arms and seven jeweled anklets about each ankle. Treasure was found in the tomb, and on a tablet at her head she had caused to be written the following inscription (the translation by Mr. Forster is reproduced by Mr. William Jones, F.S.A.):

"In thy name, O God, the God of Himyar,
I, Tajah, the daughter of Dzu Shefarr, sent my servant to Joseph,
And he, delaying to return to me, I sent my handmaid,
With a measure of silver, to bring me back a measure of flour:
And not being able to procure it, I sent her with a measure of gold:

And not being able to procure it, I commanded them to the ground:
And finding no profit in them, I am shut up here.
Whosoever may hear of it, let him pity me:
And should any woman adorn herself with an ornament
From my ornaments, may she die with no other than my death."

It would be very unlikely that after understanding these last words of the Princess Tajah (a name which quabalistically would imply "the sacrifice") any woman would be bold enough to attempt to put on the seven ropes of dead pearls and the other jewels that adorned the mortal remains of the famine-stricken princess.

Turning to later times, Benvenuto Cellini tells in his interesting memoirs a rather amusing story of a string of pearls which the Duke of Florence purchased for the duchess from "that scoundrel Bernardini" for several thousand crowns. Princess Catherine Radziwill, whose intimacy with the old courts of Europe is well known, tells of the love of the Russian Empress Marie Alexandrovna (grandmother of the unfortunate Nicholas II), for pearls which she never tired of buying. Her ropes of from 25 to 30 pearls were of varied lengths, and when worn, extended from the top to the hem of her dress. She was reputed to have had some of the largest pear-shaped pearls in the world.

James Bruce, the famous traveler (*Travels to Discover the Sources of the Nile*, 1768-1773), writes that the pinna or wing shell mentioned by Pliny, which is found with its fiber-like rope on the bed of the Red Sea, yields the beautiful pink-tinted pearl so highly prized in ancient and modern times. Red or rose-colored pearls are termed by the natives Sohitamukti. Marco Polo mentions that they are found off the island of Chipangu, "big, round and rosy, and quite as valuable as white ones." He also writes that when a dead body is burned one of these pearls is always put in the mouth, "for such is their custom." Pearls of this tint are accounted as precious objects and were used in Buddhist ceremonies and worship.

Julius Caesar was extremely fond of pearls. Caius Suetonius (*Lives of the Caesars*), tells us that he was a great expert and knew so much about them that he could estimate their exact weights "by his hand alone." The same writer tells us that Caesar's love of pearls was the cause of his expedition against Britain, the pearls he obtained there being, greatly to his chagrin, of poor quality and little luster. Nevertheless, we are told he consecrated a breastplate set with British pearls to the temple of Venus Genetrix. It is recorded that Caesar gave Servilia, the mother of Brutus, a pearl worth nearly 50,000 pounds sterling. Pearls in the time of the Caesars were the rage in Rome, and women adorned themselves lavishly with them. This custom drew violent protests from the philosopher Seneca who, alluding to a lady who wore several pearls dangling from each ear, told her husband that his wife "carried all the wealth of his house in her ears."

In the extravagant intoxication of the rich banquet which Cleopatra VII (Tryphena the Great) gave to the honor of Mark Anthony, it is related that

HOROSCOPE OF   MARY OF SCOTLAND

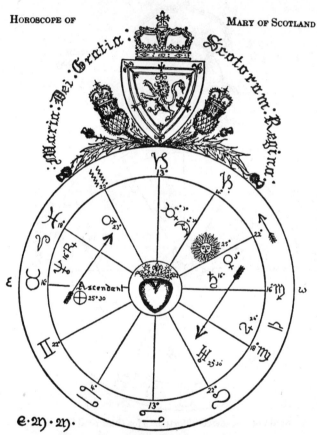

Pearls would be considered unfortunate for these rival Queens.

this queen—the last of the Ptolemies—throwing one of her valuable pearls into a vinegar solution, swallowed it. The value of this gem is set down as 80,729 pounds sterling. Its companion afterwards graced the statue of the Pantheon Venus at Rome. Cleopatra was not alone in this act of folly, for we are informed that Clodius, son of Aesopus the actor, swallowed a pearl valued at 8,072 pounds sterling. Caligula, the Roman Emperor, added this act also to his many acts of stupidity. He too enjoyed the reputation of a "pearl swallower," which title in the reign of Queen Elizabeth was also coveted by Sir Thomas Gresham who quaffed off a large pearl at a banquet which the Queen attended after visiting the Royal Exchange. The poet Heywood alludes to this act in the lines:

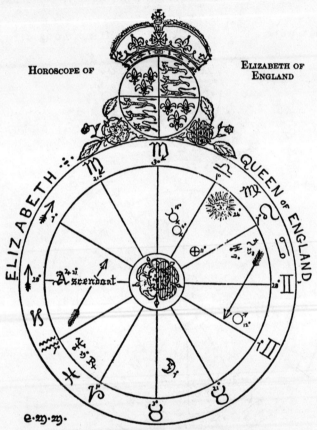

HOROSCOPE OF   ELIZABETH OF
                                ENGLAND

Pearls would be considered unfortunate for these rival Queens.

"Here 15,000 pounds at one clap goes
   Instead of sugar: Gresham drinks the pearl
   Unto his Queen and mistress."

Neither pearls nor diamonds were fortunate for Mary Queen of Scots, yet she wore both in profusion. Her wedding dress at her marriage with Philip of Spain is described as being "richly bordered with great pearls and diamonds," while she wore the great diamond which Philip had sent to her by the Marquis de las Traves. Mary's nativity favored few jewels but none less than diamonds, pearls, and rubies. History relates that, when in the days of her sorrows, the Scottish Queen was held captive by the rapacious Earl of Moray. This man, who owed her so much, sent her exquisite parure of pearls and other costly jewels to Queen Elizabeth at London.

Madame de Barrera gives the following extract from a letter of Bodutel la Forrest, French ambassador at the English court, which describes the pearl parure: "There are six cordons of large pearls strung as pater nosters: but there are five and twenty separate from the rest, much finer and larger than those which are strung: these are for the most part like black muscades." Elizabeth, after obtaining various expert opinions as to the value of this ornament, eventually purchased it at her own price. But if pearls, fortunate for Scotland, were unfortunate for Mary (for whom Scotland itself was unfortunate), they were doubly so for Elizabeth who had the dark planet Saturn and the subtle Uranus in the sign Cancer at her birth. The two famous diamond rings of Mary and Elizabeth and Elizabeth and Essex are stated to have been the indirect cause of the deaths of both Mary and Elizabeth.

Old Hebraic legend tells that manna fell from Heaven, accompanied by showers of pearls and precious stones. In ancient Judaea, it was believed that a pearl wrapped in a bag of leather and tied around the neck of oxen would benefit them and increase their fruitfulness. The Arabs sang that "Nisan's Ram (Sun in Aries) brings pearls to the sea and wheat to the land." In China the pearl was regarded as the true symbol of ability, and so the Chinese character for Pearl (Tehm) was placed on the vases used by artists, poets, scientists, and writers; and the term Tchm Onan is translated as indicating a rare pearl object. Great virtues were ascribed to the pearl by the Chinese. It was, and still is, used medicinally by them as a remedy for blood disorders, swooning, heart troubles, digestive irregularities, and stomach complaints. The ancients used pearls, we are told, as absorbents or antacids, and pearls were given to the weak-minded Charles VI of France in distilled water to cure his insanity. Dissolved in acids they were taken as an absorbent medicine and, as one writer puts it, "for the purpose of displaying the careless opulence and luxury of their possessors."

The pearl was sacred to the Angel Gabriel in the East, and amongst the Mohammedans a great white pearl—the Pearl of Paradise—reached from East to West, from Heaven to Earth. This is the Eternal Table of the Koran on which Allah has written all that has been, all that is, and all that is to come. The Arabian Heavenly Home of Glory and the Everlasting Eden of Wonder is, it is related, rich with red pearls.

Tourmaline

CHAPTER IX

PEARL

The Bishop of Chiapa Champions the Indian Pearl Divers: Size of the Old
Pearl Fields: Value of Exports to Europe in 16th Century: The Persian
Gulf: The Ceylon Fisheries: The "Binder of Sharks": The Pearl Charm of
the Divers: Classification of Pearls in Ceylon: The Red Sea Fisheries, the
Source of Cleopatra's Pearls: The Australian Fisheries: Need for their
Protection: Other Fisheries: Story of the Discovery of New Guinea Pearls:
Town of the Nymphs: River Fisheries: A River Pearl in the British Crown:
"Shells of the Flood": Divers Beneath the Sea: The Folk Lore of the Pearl:
Vishnu's Necklace of Five Precious Stones: Emblems of Pearls: Pearls and
Persons: Pearls and Lunar Numbers: A Madagascar Birth Custom: The
Angel, Day, Sign, and Planet of the Pearl: As a Dream Symbol: Prejudice
and Its Value: The Pearls of Linnaeus: Chinese and Japanese Culture
Pearls: Pearl "Faking": Coconut Pearls.

> "Or where the gorgeous East with richest hand
> Showers on her Kings barbaric pearl and gold."
> Milton

The benevolent Bishop of Chiapa, Mexico, Bartolome de las Casas,
came forth as the protector of the Indians in the cruel times of their oppression. On their behalf he crossed the Atlantic 16 times, and he tells of the
hellish tortures to which they were subjected by their Spanish conquerors.
"Nothing," says this good man, "nothing could be more cruel and more
detestable" (*Brevissima Relacion de la Destruccion de las Indias,* 1539).
The story he writes of the Indian pearl divers is a sad one. As soon as the
diver came up from the depths the brutal overseer, scarcely allowing him
time to breathe the pure air, beat him savagely and compelled him to go
down again. His food was poor and scanty, and Mother Earth his bed.
His glossy black hair turned prematurely gray, his lungs became diseased,
he spat blood freely, and the ravenous shark ended his tragic life on earth.

The natural result of greed and oppression practically exhausted these fisheries from the neighborhood of which the ancient kings of Mexico drew so much wealth. Indeed, it was the sight of the poor natives adorned with ropes of pearls which excited the cupidity of the first Spaniards who adventured to their shores. There being no provision made for the protection of the oysters in this fishery, it "gave out" almost entirely towards the end of the 17th century.

An idea of the magnitude of these fisheries (which included the ancient grounds between Acapulco and the Gulf of Tehuantepec on the West Mexican coast, and the Caribbean Sea by the islands of Coche, Cubagua, and Margarita) can be gathered from the value of the export to Europe in the first half of the 16th century. The annual value exported was stated to exceed 800,000 Spanish dollars, those famous "Pieces of Eight" which bring us back to the time of *Treasure Island* and the buccaneers of the Spanish Main. As much as 700 pounds of pearls were sent to Seville in the year 1587, amongst them, it is stated, being specimens of rare worth and beauty. Fine quality pearls are still found at Panama and the Gulf of Mexico. The poor progress of these fisheries is said to be due to the wretched pay offered to the Indian and Negro divers in the past. It is a strange fact that progress and prosperity are gained only by the pursuance of an enlightened policy towards employees, and this is nowhere so clearly indicated as in the history of the pearl.

Pearls from the Persian Gulf are amongst the most esteemed of the present day. The fisheries of the Great Pearl Bank extend west from Ras Hassan half way up the Gulf. To the Eastern, no pearl is so beautiful and full of color as the pearl from the Persian Gulf. The color is very enduring and improves by being worn next to the skin—especially of a person whose jewel it is.

The Ceylon fisheries have not been yielding so well of late years, but with wisdom will no doubt regain their old place. The main oyster bank is near Condatchy, about 20 miles from the shore. Twenty men, ten of whom are divers, under a tindal, or captain, comprise the crew of each boat. The divers are quick and expert at their work, and although remaining under water seldom more than a minute, have been known to bring to the surface as many as 150 shells. The pearl diver's greatest dread is the ground shark, and all the time the boats are out the conjurer, termed the "Binder of Sharks" or "Pillal Harras," stands on the shore muttering prayers and conjurations. The divers also wear a pearl about their bodies as a charm against their dreaded enemy. The beautiful island of Ceylon— the Taprobane of the old Greeks and Romans and the Serendib of the Arabian Nights—is itself shaped like a great drop pearl and is believed by the Indians to be a "part of Paradise."

Perfectly round and fine luster pearls are called by the Ceylonese "annees," next in grade are called "annadaree." Irregular pearls of lesser luster are called "kayarel," generally known amongst us as "baroques." Pearl-shaped inferior specimens are called "samadiem," those duller and irregular are termed "kallipoo," a poorer grade again is known as "koorwell," and the lowest type is "pesul." Small seed pearls are known as "tool."

Cleopatra's famous pearls no doubt came from the Red Sea fisheries which are believed to have been the property of the Egyptian rulers. The Western Australian fisheries, especially those at Broome and Shark's Bay, are becoming of greater importance and value, although judicious and scientific means should be taken to prevent these valuable fields from sharing the fate of some of the older ones. The fisheries at Thursday Island and Northern Australia are important, and the author was told that pearls were discovered in New Guinea through a sailor's row with the natives, who pelted the offending lugger with pearl-bearing shells which, when broken on the decks of the vessel, revealed their precious prizes.

The remarkable Town of the Nymphs near the Japanese city of Ishinomonsky on the Pacific coast, obtains its name from the women who support their families by diving for pearls. The town is many centuries old, and the nymphs begin their strenuous work at the age of 14, continuing until they are 40. Pearl shells abound in Sebiam Bay, and the nymphs work ten hours a day in summer time. The length of each immersion is from two to three minutes. When the baby girl is four years of age she is taken to the sea and taught to swim and dive. These lessons continue until the time comes for the serious practice of the pearl seekers' profession. This work is all done by women, while the men attend to the training of the children and the duties of the household.

Mention may also be made of the river fisheries of England, Scotland, Wales, Ireland, and various parts of Europe. However, the pearls found are as a rule not of great importance, although it is stated that Sir Richard Wynn of Gwydyr, Chamberlain to Catherine, wife of Charles II, sent a pearl from the river Conway in North Wales as a present to the Queen, which pearl is today in the King of England's crown. In Wales, these river pearl shells are called by the poetic name cregin y dylu, "shells of the Flood."

The gradual replacement of naked divers by those in diving dress may tend to make the yields more effective, but the work is not without its dangers, the toiler beneath the sea having still to meet the challenge of its denizens—the shark, the diamond fish, and the deadly octopus.

"The Kingdom of Heaven is like unto a merchantman seeking
 goodly pearls."

Book of Matthew

The pearl was esteemed as the emblem of purity, innocence, and
peace, and was sacred to the Moon and Diana. For this reason in ancient
times it was worn by young girls and virgins on whom the protection of
"chaste Diana" was invoked. Generally as an emblem of chastity the pearl
was worn on the neck. As a cure for irritability it was ground to a fine
powder and a quantity, seldom more than a grain, was drunk in new milk.
In doses of the same quantity mixed with sugar, it was recommended to be
taken as a charm against the pestilence.

The Hindus included the pearl amongst the five precious stones in the
magical necklace of Vishnu, the other four being the diamond, ruby,
emerald, and sapphire. The golden pearl was the emblem of wealth, the
white of idealism, the black of philosophy, the pink of beauty, the red of
health and energy, and the gray of thought. Lusterless pearls are considered unfortunate, as are pearls that have lost their sheen when on a dying
person's finger, as sometimes happens.

It is curious how pearls improve in luster when worn by some persons
and how they deteriorate when worn by others. A recent writer comment-
ing on this advised that if "pearls turned colour temporarily when worn by
certain persons they should be put away for a few days and the detrimental
effects of constitutional acids will be found to have entirely disappeared."
To an extent this is correct, but it is equally certain that if the person by
whom the pearls were affected were to continue wearing them they would
be destroyed altogether. This is quite in accord with the occult philosophy
of the ancient masters, who held that only people who had favorable planets in Cancer—the celestial sign of the Ocean—or in whose nativities the
lunar aspects were favorable could wear pearls. The Moon, however, in
the sign Capricorn was not considered favorable for wearing pearls, and
some writers also include the sign Scorpio. A half-moon shaped whitish
stone of about 25 pounds weight was oftentimes used by the Ceylonese
pearl divers, tied around their wrists, when making the plunge for the
pearl oyster, and the crew of 20—a lunar number—which made up the
Ceylon pearling boat company may have traditional authority, and may be
something more than mere coincidence.

The Princess of Yemen, previously mentioned, wore seven strands of
pearls. Seven is the positive number of the Moon or the Moon's number
when going from new to full. This was recognized by ancient nations,
and it may be well assumed that the symbolic meaning was understood by
the advisers to the Princess.

A custom exists in Madagascar which finds a parallel amongst the ancients. It is believed that if, at an afflicted birth, pearls are buried, good will come to the child and will continue to come unless the pearls be unearthed.

The pearl was sacred to the Angel Gabriel, and Monday was its special day of the week. The Moon was its planet and the zodiacal Cancer its sign. To dream of pearls is considered a favorable omen, being held to indicate wealth and honor gained by personal exertion. To the poor, the pearl denotes riches. It is the symbol of happy marriage and popularity. That pearls are unfortunate is as untrue as that opals or any other gems are. That they are unfavorable to some is as true as that they are favorable to others, but prejudice is hard to kill. A young lady of good family actually told the author that she would never wear pearls because she was unfortunate whenever she wore her necklace. Upon examining this terrible necklace, the author saw that the alleged pearls were merely imitation!

As imitation pearls scarcely come within the province of this book it may be sufficient to mention that in the year 1748 Linnaeus wrote to Dr. Haller, the physiologist, telling him that he had ascertained how pearls grow in shells. "I am able to produce in any mother of pearl shell that can be held in the hand, in the course of four or five years, a pearl as large as the seed of a common vetch." This discovery by the great naturalist was regarded as of such importance by the Swedish government that they ennobled Linnaeus, rewarded him with a gift of 450 pounds, and began to manufacture pearls under his direction with great secrecy. Linnaeus' method had long been anticipated by the Chinese, who used to throw pieces of mother of pearl and grit into the live oyster. It is said that in a year the coating over a piece of mother of pearl would be sufficient. Of late years the Japanese have acted on these practices with considerable skill, producing by mechanial means some beautiful specimens. Still, beautiful as they are, they are not *real* pearls.

A good deal of pearl "faking" is practiced, and a short time ago a pearl broker in Paris was sentenced to imprisonment for tampering with the color of a pearl. But whenever chemical means are employed in tinting a pearl, the false colors invariably fade and leave the specimen worse off than before, more especially if a lady with a "good pearl skin" wears it.

In his book *Malay Magic*, Mr. W. W. Satek gives the following interesting account of "coconut pearls," quoting from Dr. Deny's *Descriptive Dictionary of British Malaysia*, with acknowledgements to nature.

"During my recent travels," Dr. Sidney Hickson writes to a scientific contemporary, "I was frequently asked by Dutch planters and others if I had ever seen a 'cocoanut stone.' These stones are said to be rarely found (one in two thousand or more) in the perisperm of the cocoanut, and when found are kept by the natives as a charm against disease and evil spirits. This story of the cocoanut stone was so constantly told me, and in every case without variations in its details, that I made every effort before leaving to obtain some specimens and eventually succeeded in obtaining two. One of these is nearly a perfect sphere, 14 mm in diameter, and the other, rather smaller in size, is irregularly pear-shaped. In both specimens the surface is worn nearly smooth by friction. The spherical one I have had cut into two halves, but I can find no concentric or other markings on the polished cut surface. Dr. Kimmins has kindly submitted a half to a careful chemical analysis and finds that it consists of pure carbonate of lime without any trace of other salts or vegetable tissue." On this letter Mr. Thistleton Dyer remarks:

"Dr. Hickson's account of the calcareous concretions occasionally found in the central hollow—filled with fluid—of the endosperm of the seed of the cocoanut is extremely interesting. The circumstances of the occurrence of these stones or pearls are in many respects parallel to those which attend the formation of tabasheer. In both cases mineral matter in palpable masses is withdrawn from solution in considerable volumes of flint contained in tolerably large cavities in living plants and in both instances they are monocotyledons. In the case of coconut pearls the material is calcium carbonate and this is well known to concrete in a peculiar manner from solutions in which organic matter is also present. In my note on Tabasheer I referred to the reported occurrence of mineral concretions in the wood of various tropical dicotyledonous trees. Tabasheer is too well known to be pooh-poohed, but some of my scientific friends express a polite incredulity in the other cases."

The specimen presented by Mr. Skeat to the Cambridge Ethnological Museum is encircled by a black ring which is caused, it is said, by its adherence to the shell of the coconut. These coconut pearls are of much interest and may perhaps be included amongst the mineral curiosities which comprehend tabasheer and apatite. Ancient philosophy would probably associate them with the sign Cancer, as is the case with pearls found in seas and rivers. Swedenborg writes that pearls are truth and the knowledge of truth, celestial and spiritual knowledge, faith and charity.

CHAPTER X

PERIDOT-RUBY

Peridot: Plasma: The Rewarding Hermes: Porphyry, Its Introduction into Rome By Vitrasius Pollio: Prase or Mother of Emerald: Pyrite: The Pyrites Lithos of Isidore of Seville: A Primitive Firestone: Used for Firearms: The "Seed of Minerals": Mundic of the Miners: Its Change to Vitriol in Mining Districts: Spinon of Theophrastus: French "Pierre De Sante": Marcasite Used as a Jewel Ornament: Eden's Flowers of Metals: Pyrope: Quartz: Rubellite: Rubicelle: Ruby, The Corundum Family: The Term "Oriental": The Mogok Mines: "Lord of the Rubies": The Mine Eaters: "The Dragon Lord": The King of Scilan's Ruby: Cosmas Indicopleustes: A Coronation Custom Described by Hatyon: Tears of Buddha: The Ruby Bowl of Arya Chakravarti: Colonel Alexander Gardener and the Fakir's Ruby: The King of Vishapoor's Ruby: Rubies Placed Under the Foundations of Buildings: Rubies in the Cho Keng Su: Pliny's Acausti: Practice of the Ethiopians: Anthrax of Theophrastus: Duke of Devonshire's Ruby: Rubies Mentioned by Mr. C. W. King: Rabbi Ragiel's Talisman: Dragons Guardians of Ruby Mines: M. Rochefort's Story and the Ruby in the Dragon's Head: St. Margaret and the Dragon: Sheikh El Mohdy and the Ruby-Jewelled Dragon: Barthoveri and the Serpent: Dieudonne of Gozon and the Dragon of Rhodes: The Import of These Legends: St. George and St. Michael and the Dragons: Shrine of the Magi in Cologne Cathedral: The Sun and Christianity: The Names of the Magi: The Rosicrucian Classification: The "Regale" of France, from the Tomb of St. Thomas A'Becket, Worn by Henry VIII: Vow of Louis VII of France and Its Fulfillment at Canterbury: Swedenborg's Correspondence of the Ruby: Comtesse D'Anois' Story of the Ruby Singing Apple: The Arabs and the Angel of the World: Persian Charm Against the Forces of Evil: The Fourth Stone of the Nao-Rattan: Burmese Symbol of Reincarnation: A Ruby Which Nearly Destroyed a Native State in India: Jeweled Rings on the Statue of St. Lambert at Liege Cathedral: Catharine of Aragon Reads Misfortune in Her Ruby's Change of Color: Occult Virtues of the Ruby: Symbol of the Ruby in Dreams:

Color Phenomena Displayed By a Ruby: The Star Ruby: The Hunter and the Ruby.

PERIDOT: (see Chrysolite)

PLASMA: This variety of leek-green jasper is derived from the Greek word plasma, an image. It was a favorite stone among the ancients who employed it in gem engraving and for important talismans. In the Rhodes collection there is a beautiful oval specimen on which is engraved a nude figure of Hermes holding a caduceus in his left hand, while on his right above a purse is perched a cock; a scorpion is on his left side, a little above his knee. He wears the winged cap on his head. Mr. King classes this piece as astrological. It symbolizes the wisdom and rewards of the well-starred subject of Mercury. Plasma was largely used in Abraxus charms by the Gnostics who employed the substance always for special talismans. Astrologically, plasma is under the zodiacal Virgin.

PORPHYRY: The name is derived from the Greek word for purple—porphyra, and we find it written at various periods in many ways, for example: porfurie, porphurye, purphire, porpherie, and porphiry. It is a hard purple and white stone said to have been introduced into Rome by Vitrasisus Pollio in the form of statues of Claudius. The quarries whence the ancients obtained their supplies of porphyry were found at Gebel Dokhan near the Red Sea by Wilkinson and Burton. It has always been a favorite stone with sculptors, glyptic artists, and architects, and was chiefly esteemed in the forming of columns. Porphyry was regarded as a stone to promote eloquence in speaking. Astrologically, it was placed under "the sign of the Columns," Gemini.

PRASE: The name is derived from the Greek prason, a leek. Leonardus calls it prassius, and he says it is so termed from an herb of its own name. It is also written as prasius or prasium. It is thus described by Marbodus:

> "Midst precious stones a place the Prase may claim,
>   Of value small, content with beauty's fame.
>   No virtue has it: but it brightly gleams
>   With emerald green, and well the gold beseems;
>   Or blood-red spots diversify its green,
>   Or crossed with three white lines its face is seen."

Other authors, however, endow the prase with a virtue. It was regarded by some as a beauty charm for married women and for the mothers of brides. It resembles the beryl in its clear form, but it is duller. It is translucent and, as its name indicates, leek-green in color. At one time it was believed to be the matrix of the emerald, whence it was called "Mother of Emerald." It is under the zodiacal Taurus.

PYRITE:

> "Named from the fire the yellow pyrite spurns
> The touch of man, and to be handled scorns:
> Touch it with trembling hand and cautious arm
> For, tightly grasped, it burns the closed palm."

The word is found also as pyrit and pirrite, and old writers of the 16th century were especially fond of using pyrit stone. It is derived from the Greek pur, fire, and is allied to the fire stone family (pyrites lithos) noted by Isidore of Seville (6th and 7th centuries) in his philosophical fragments from the more ancient writers. He identifies the black pyrites of Pliny in a black Persian stone which, if fractured, and held in the hand, burns. It is assumed from the frequent occurrence of pieces of pyrites in prehistoric mounds that primitive man used the substance for kindling fires. Later we find it employed before the introduction of flint in wheel lock fire arms when, in the same manner, it threw out sparks of fire when energetically struck on steel.

The ancients had a theory that pyrite was the seed or original matter of minerals, and we find it in rocks of every age. To mining people it is known as mundic. Auriferous pyrite, which occurs in auriferous countries, contains certain quantities of gold, sometimes worth winning, and was known as King of the Pyrites. The action of water and air makes it troublesome in coal-mining districts. It is then changed into sulphate of iron (vitriol) and fires the mines. Chambers (1866) mentions that "at Quarreltown in Renfrewshire a deep hollow may still be seen where about a century ago the ground fell in consequence of a subterranean fire thus kindled."

Theophrastus, the great Greek naturalist and philosopher of the 3rd century before the Christian era, mentions in his work on stones the burning pyrite under the name spinon which, he says, is contained in certain mines and which, if crushed, watered, and exposed to the rays of the sun, bursts into flame. The French call this stone Pierre de Sante (Stone of Health), because it was said that it is affected by the health of the wearer.

The white iron pyrite, known as marcasite, is of similar composition to the ordinary pyrite (iron disulphide), but it takes on the orthorhombic form of crystallization instead of the usual cube form. This word is also found written as markasit and marquesite. The stone was largely used for jewel ornamentation. Oliver Goldsmith, in *She Stoops to Conquer,* says, "Half the ladies of our acquaintance carry their jewels to town and bring nothing but paste and marcasites back." Eden in 1555 wrote that "Marchasites are flowers of metals by the colours where of the kyndes of metals are known." Mr. William Jones mentions a ring in the possession of a clergyman which is made of two hearts surmounted by a crown set with marcasites. Rabbi Chael says that a man on horseback holding a bridle and bent bow engraved on pyrites makes the wearer irresistable in war. These stones are martial according to astrology and are attached to the zodiacal Scorpio.

PYROPE: (see Garnet)

QUARTZ: In 1772 Cronstedt wrote in his work on mineralogy: "I shall adopt the name of Quartz in English as it has already general access in other European Languages." There seems to be little doubt regarding the origin of the word which comes from the German quarz. Professor James D. Dana gives the quartz varieties under the following heads:

1. Vitreous. Distinguished by their glassy fracture.
2. Chalcedonic. Having a subvitreous or a waxy luster and generally translucent.
3. Jaspery Cryptocrystalline. Having barely a glimmering luster or none, and opaque.

To the first belong: Amethyst, aventurine quartz, cairngorm, citrine, ferruginous quartz, false or Spanish topaz, milk quartz, prase, rock crystal, rose quartz, and smoky quartz.

To the second belong: Chalcedony, chrysoprase, sard, carnelian, agate, onyx, cat's eye, flint, hornstone, chert, and plasma.

To the third belong: Jasper, heliotrope or bloodstone, lydian stone, touchstone, basanite, silicified wood, and pseudomorphous quartz.

Opal is a near ally to quartz which is a most useful as well as an ornamental substance.

RUBELLITE: (see Tourmaline)

RUBICELLE: (see Spinel)

RUBY:

"He that has once the flower of the Sunne
The perfect ruby which we call elixir."
Ben Johnson

The ruby derives its name from the Latin ruber, red, and some of its forms at various periods are given by Dr. Murray as rubye, rubie, rubey, roby, rooby, rube, rubu, rybe, rybee, rybwe, ribe, and riby. The stone is of the corundum family which includes the sapphire, oriental amethyst, oriental topaz, oriental chrysoberyl, oriental emerald, oriental cat's eye, oriental moonstone, adamantine spar of hair-brown color and the well-known emery. The term "oriental" is also applied to the ruby and serves to distinguish it from the spinel, ruby, garnet, and a number of other red stones. The definition "oriental" is applied only to the corundum family and was, according to Dr. G. F. H. Smith, attached to these hard colored stones which in early days reached Europe by way of the East.

The name "corundum" is derived from a Sanskrit word of doubtful meaning, and the minerals included in it come next in hardness to the diamond. The ruby therefore is a red sapphire, and the sapphire a blue ruby, and it is no infrequent thing to find the two stones combined in one specimen. Mr. Emanuel has drawn attention to the fact that rubies and sapphires are always found in gold-bearing country. It has been stated that, while sapphires have been found in Australia, the red sapphire or ruby has not. This is incorrect. At the Anakie sapphire fields in Central Queensland rubies are also found, and some specimens exhibit blended colors. It is true, however, that rubies have not up to the present been found in Australia in great quantities.

The most celebrated ruby mines in the world are the Mogok mines in Upper Burma. Here the stones are found in calcite deposits occurring in granular limestone on the hillsides and in the clayey alluvial deposits of the river beds. These workings are of very great age and, until 1885, were the monopoly of the Burmese Crown, the King being known as Lord of the Rubies. In this country the ruby fields are called "byon," and the miners "twin-tsas" (mine eaters). These twin-tsas were forced to surrender to the monarch all big stones found by them, which stones were carefully guarded in the Royal Treasure House. One of the mine eaters found a large and beautiful gem which, in order to escape the selfish conditions imposed, he divided into two parts; one of these he handed over to the officers of the King, the other he endeavored to conceal. The plot it seems failed, with what result to the unfortunate "eater" is not told. The weight of these two sections after the cutter had exerted his skill on them was 98 and 74 carats. A fine Burma ruby called "Gnaga Boh," or the Dragon Lord (the folklore of the East connects rubies and dragons) weighed over 40 carats, losing about half in the cutting. The uncut part of the Great Burmese Ruby (a stone that weighed 400 carats and was split into three parts, two of which were cut) was sold in Calcutta for seven lakhs of rupees (at the exchange rate of two shillings English for the rupee a lakh would equal 10,000 pounds).

Marco Polo wrote of the great ruby possessed by the King of the Island of Seilan (Ceylon), "The finest and biggest in the world. . . .It is about a palm in length and as thick as a man's arm: to look at, it is the most resplendent object upon earth: it is quite free from flaw and is as red as fire. Its value is so great that a price for it in money could not be named. The great Kaan sent an embassy and begged the King as a favour to sell this to him offering to give for it the ransom of a city or, in fact, what the King would. But the King replied that on no account whatever would he sell it for it had come to him from his ancestors."

The great merchant-traveler Cosmas Indicopleustes of Alexandria, wrote in his *Voyages* (1666) of this stone, which "they say is of great size and brilliant ruddy hue, as large as a giant pine cone. When seen flashing from afar—especially if the Sun's rays flood upon it—it is a sight both marvellous and unequalled." Hayton, his contemporary, also wrote of this wonderful stone: "At the King of the Island of Ceylon's coronation he places this ruby in his left hand and rides thus with it throughout his city, after which all know him as their king and obey him as such." The Chinese writer Hyuen Tsang also told of this great stone, as did Odoric. Friar Jordamus discoursed not only of this but of the great and wonderful rubies in the possession of the Island King. Andrea Corsali (1515) also described the King of Sylen's (Ceylon) two great rubies—"so shining and sparkling as to seem like flames of fire." In the Ceylon river beds fine rubies are discovered, and old writers say that many are washed down from the mountain "which they call Adam's Peak." There was superstitious belief in the beautiful Island of Ceylon that rubies are the consolidated tears of Buddha.

One of the great medieval Tamul chiefs, Arya Chakravarti, had, it is said, a ruby bowl the size of the palm of a man's hand which was remarkable for its brilliant color. Colonel Alexander Gardner, Colonel of Artillery in the service of Maharaja Ranyit Singh, describes a visit he made with the Bai or Baron of the Kirghiz to a venerable aged fakir whose worldly possessions seemed to consist of earthen pots of grain placed in a hole in the middle of his hut. The old philosopher was the reputed possessor of a rare and beautiful ruby. For this the Bai entreated the silent and unmoved fakir, declaring that with it alone could he induce the robber chief he was traveling to see to spare "the lives, property, and honour of all the innocent families around." At last the fakir quietly arose, and after a little fumbling produced the gem which, with a dignified gesture, he placed softly in the Bai's hands, giving him his blessing and expressing the hope that the offering might have the desired result, after which he relapsed into silent reverie. He declined money for the gem, asking only that some grain might be sent him so "that he might be able to relieve way-worn and destitute travelers."

The Colonel examined the gem and found cut in high relief on the center of the oblong face of the stone a small Zoroastrian altar. Round this altar were double cordons of letters similar to those appearing on the Scytho Bactrian coins. The Colonel describes the gem as pure and lustrous, of great value, and from 150 to 200 carats in weight. This rare gem was discovered at the time of Timur by an ancestor of the fakir in a cave near the famous shrine of the city of Esh or Oosh on the Bolor Ranges.

A fine ruby of 50 carats which belonged to the King of Vishapoor is mentioned by Tavernier. In China the ruby has always been esteemed, and its primary importance as a distinguishing emblem in the cap of the Chief Mandarin has already been noted. A specimen was also placed under the foundations of a building of importance "to give it a good destiny." In the Chinese work *Cho Keng Lu,* which relates to various affairs up to the Mongol dynasty, deep red rubies are termed "si-la-ni." Scholars translate this word as "from Ceylon." They are also known as "hung pao shi" (precious red stone) and "chin chu." It has a sacred meaning and talismanic virtue and is attached to the dress set in rare jade and employed as a precious ornament.

Pliny calls rubies "acausti" and says that they are not injured by fire. He relates a practice of Ethopian merchants of placing a ruby in a vinegar solution for two weeks to improve its luster. The effect was, it is said, good for a short period of time, but ultimately the stones became soft and fragile. The anthrax or "glowing coal" of Theophrastus is identified as the ruby as we know it today. He gives us an idea of the money value of this stone by stating that a very small specimen would sell for forty golden staters (a gold stater is worth about five dollars in the United States). Amongst the gems collected in the 18th century by William, third Duke of Devonshire, there is a ruby of about three carats weight, described by Mr. King as of "the most delicious cerise colour" on which are cut deeply the figures of Venus and Cupid. The work is of the middle Roman Period, and Mr. King deplores the fact that the great value of the gem was in his opinion injured by the inferiority of the workmanship. A Faun's Head on an inferior ruby in the same collection is superior from an art point of view and of greater age. Mr. King mentions a beautiful rose-colored ruby of irregular form on which is a magnificent head of Thetis wearing a crab's shell helmet of most exquisite Greek work. Rabbi Ragiel (*Book of Wings*) writes that the figure of a dragon cut on a ruby increases the worldly possessions of the wearer, giving happiness and ease.

Old legends say that the ruby mines as well as the emerald mines were guarded by dragons, and the symbolic connection between the dragon, and the ruby has the virtue of far-reaching antiquity. M. Rochefort in his *Natural History of the Antilles,* says that the Caribbees of Dominica speak of a dragon which lives in a declivity of the rocks and in whose head is a giant ruby so brilliant that the surrounding country is illumined by it. These people believed that the Son of God came out of the heavens to slay the dragon. St. Margaret is said to have subdued a dragon and to have taken a wonderful ruby from its head. The Arabian writer Sheikh El Mohdy has amongst his stories one telling of a terrible dragon which inhabited the island of Ceylon and carried in his head a large ruby which shone for many miles amidst the darkness of night. The Indian philosopher Barthoveri said that "the serpent is malefic although it carries a ruby in its head." Dieudonne of Goyon is said to have killed a terrible dragon at Rhodes and to have drawn from its head a wonderful iridescent stone the size of an olive.

Some few writers substitute the diamond for the ruby, but whether we take the many-colored stone of Dieudonne (which it has been said was a diamond) or the stones of the Sun, the ruby and the diamond, the import of the legends are similar. The dragon as the symbol of the lower forces whether as the poisonous emanations of stagnant waters or as the Serpent of Eden—the planet Mars and one of his heavenly Houses, Scorpio, or the planet Saturn and his heavenly House, Capricorn—is continually exposed to the benefic rays of the Sun. These rays are personified by the contests between the Sun-Angel Michael and the dragon and our well-known St. George.

The three skulls, said to be the skulls of the "Three Kings" in the jewelled "Shrine of the Magi" in Cologne Cathedral, have their names Melchior, Gaspar, and Balthazar worked on them in rubies, perhaps because the Sun, planet of the ruby, was the accredited planet of Christianity as noted by Albertus Magnus and the Cardinal Dailly. The names of the Magi have also been given as Megalath, Galgatlath and Sarasin, Apellius, Amerus and Damascus, and Ator, Sator and Peratoras. In their allegories the Rosicrucians follow very nearly the names on the skulls in the 12th century Shrine at Cologne.

Jasper or Gaspar, the white lord with a diamond
Melchior, the bright lord with a diamond
Belshazzar or Balthazar, the treasure lord with a ruby.

It is said that Henry VIII wore on his thumb a ring in which was set a ruby (some say a diamond) from the tomb of St. Thomas A'Becket. This ruby, known as the "Regale of France," was the talismanic gem of the French King Louis VII who, in accordance with a battle vow, visited the tomb at Canterbury in the year 1179. While offering his devotions he was asked by the priests at the shrine to give as an offering this beautiful jewel. Being loath to part with his talisman, the King agreed to give one hundred thousand florins in its stead, to which generous substitution the Canterbury fathers humbly agreed. But the precious ruby which dazzled all with its brightness, turning night into day, refused to be thus protected and, flying from the setting of the ring on the King's finger, fixed itself on the Saint's tomb.

Swedenborg recognizes in the ruby a gem of passionate devotion and likens it to the appearance of the Lord's Divine Sphere represented in the celestial Heavens.

In Comtesse d'Anois' fairy story *Chery and Fairstar*, there is a narrative of a ruby apple on an amber stem which is known as the "Singing Apple." This apple gave forth a perfume so weirdly sweet that it caused people to laugh or to cry, to write poems or to sing songs; but when it sang itself the hearers were transported with ecstasy. Guarded by a great three-headed dragon with 12 feet, the apple rested in the Libyan desert. The apple was acquired by Prince Chery. The reflections of his glass armour terrified the dragon and drove it into a cave, the entrance to which was securely shut up by the victor.

The Arabs say that the Angel Bearer of the World stands on a rock of pure ruby, and amongst the Persians the gem was used in magical rites as a charm against the Black Forces. It was the fourth stone of the Nao-Rattan which Iarchus gave to Apollonius, representing Benevolence, Charity, Divine Power, and Dignity. The Burmese value the ruby as an especially sacred stone which to them is a symbol of the last incarnation which precedes the final embrace of Divinity. The beautiful ruby is likened to rich ripe fruit, and its magical power is matured. It has been stated that the ruby is unfortunate for India, a country under the celestial Capricorn, and one great specimen nearly destroyed a native state, after which event it was buried with solemn ceremonies in the heart of the Himalayas.

It was an ancient custom to adorn sacred statues with precious stones, and the practice has survived into Christian times. Mr. William Jones describes a large shrine in the Liege Cathedral whereon was a figure, more than life size, of St. Lambert. On each hand were three jeweled rings, the most brilliant of which was set with a rare 10-carat ruby. The shrine was of the latter 15th and early 16th centuries. Many similar votive offerings are recorded.

For a ruby to change its color was regarded as a forerunner of misfortune, and it is said that the unhappy wife of Henry VIII, Catharine of

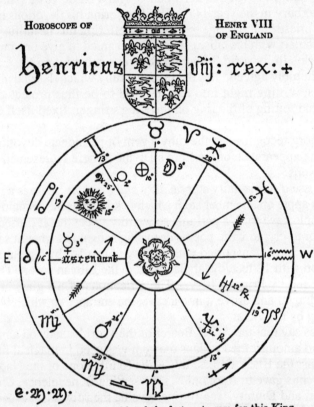

HOROSCOPE OF   HENRY VIII OF ENGLAND

The Ruby was considered the fortunate gem for this King.

Aragon, observing a change in her ruby ring, foretold her own fall. After danger has passed, old writers say, the ruby returns to its color again, if it is the true gem of the wearer.

The ruby is an emblem of passion, affection, power, and majesty. It had the reputation of attracting and retaining material love. It was probably for this reason that the amorous Henry VIII of England wore the "Regale of France." It removed obstacles, gave victory, and revealed the hidden places of stolen treasure. It signified vitality, life and happiness, and was an amulet against plagues, poison, sorrow, and evil spirits, who dreaded the flashing of the stone from the hand of a good person.

The dream of a ruby indicated to the businessman rich patronage and success in trade, to the farmer a successful harvest, and to the professional man elevation or fame and success in different degrees. It was always considered more fortunate to wear the ruby on the left hand or left side of the body. The colors of the gem vary from a light rose to a deep red, the most expensive color being that nearest to pigeon's blood. Submitted to a high temperature it turns green but when cooling returns to its original color. A particularly fortunate and rare variety is the star or asteriated ruby, which exhibits a perfect star on its beautifully rounded cabochon surface, coming as it were from a chatoyant interior. Messrs. Jerningham and Bettany in their *Bargain Book* relate how a traveler in Amazonia found, in the crop of a bird which he had shot, a large and handsome ruby which he had cut and set in a ring as a souvenir of this uncommon event. The ruby is under the celestial sign Leo.

Pyrite

CHAPTER XI

RUTILE-SAPPHIRE

Rutile: Veneris Crinis or Hair of Venus, Net of Thetis, Fleches D'Amour or Love's Arrows: Its Composition and Place in the Zodiac: Sapphire: Its Ancient Name: Male and Female: Favored Colors: The Sapphire Fields: Messrs. Rand and Dunstan on the Central Queensland Fields at Anakie: Minerals Found Associated with Sapphire: Dishonest Trade Classification: Large Sapphires: A Holy Gem: Sacred to Phoebus: Solinus and the Sign Aquarius: The Sapphire and the Eyes: Medicine Administered Astrologically: Porta on the Sapphire: Boetius and the Priestly Stone: Pope Innocent III Recommends it as a Bishop's Stone: Intaglio of Pope Paul III: St. Jerome on the Sapphire: A Stone of the People Worn by the King: King Solomon's Sapphire: Saved from the Sack of Jerusalem: The Stone of Moses: Constantine's Sapphire: Buddhists and the Sapphire: Its Place in the Nao-Rattan and the Necklace of Vishnu: Falls from the Dead Eyes of Malla Bali: Lady Scroope Throws the Sapphire Ring from the Window of Queen Elizabeth's Death Chamber: The Sepher of Solomon: The Book of Wings: Talismanic Sapphires: The Sapphire Dream: The Asteriated Sapphire: The Sapphire and the Zodiac.

RUTILE:

"Fair tresses man's imperial race ensnare,
And beauty draws us with a single hair."
Pope

The name rutile is derived from the Latin rutilus, red, and it appeared under the form rutil in 1803 when it was first applied to the mineral by Dr. A. G. Werner. The mineral occurs in brown, red, yellow, and black colors and is composed of oxygen and titanium. In hardness it is about the same as a peridot. The name Veneris Crinis (Hair of Venus) was first given to fibrilous rutile in quartz crystal known as sagenite, from a Greek word meaning "a net." The Hair of Venus was suggested by the beautiful hair-like effect which, in good specimens, is truly Titian. It is also known as The Net of Thetis and the Hair of Thetis. The French call it "Fleches d'Amour" (Love's Arrows). The Veneris Crinis was worn by the ancients as a charm to favor the growth of hair and to give foreknowledge. Rutile is under the celestial Sagittarius.

SAPPHIRE:

"The living throne, the sapphire blaze,
 Where angels tremble while they gaze."
                                        Gray

The sapphire derives its name from the Greek sappheiros, and the following are some of the many forms of the word: saphyr, saphir, safir, safire, zaphire, safere, saffere, safyre, sapher, saphyre, saphire, saffyr, saffre, safeur, safour, safur, sapheir, saphere, safure, saffure, saffoure, saufir, sapphier, saiffer, and sapphyr.

The sapphire, which may be said to lead the corundum family, is slightly harder than the ruby. The name, which varies but little in ancient languages, was without doubt applied to the blue lapis lazuli, the hyacinthus of the ancients being the true sapphire of our days. Sapphire is the name given to the blue corundum, and the shades of color vary from very light to very dark, the light specimens being anciently termed female, the dark, male. This blue tinge will, however, be detected in several light varieties of the corundum family. The velvety blue sapphire termed the "bleu du roi" has held its popularity for ages and is likely to continue to do so, although the pretty light specimens known as "cornflower blue" are fast coming into favor. Sapphires are found in Ceylon, India, and Siam in considerable quantity and some good stones have been found in the United States. Large specimens come from Newton, New Jersey, and also from the rich country around Montana. The sapphire field at Anakie, Central Queensland, bid fair to become one of the biggest in the world. In a highly instructive report, Messrs. William Rands and B. Dunstan, Government Geologists of Queensland, give a detailed account of the fields. The authors of the report give the following list of minerals found in the sapphire deposits:

Diamonds
Sapphire (blue)
Oriental Ruby (red)
Oriental Topaz (yellow)

Oriental Peridot (green)
Oriental Chrysoberyl (yellowish green)
Oriental Amethyst (purple)
Cat's Eye (smoky, etc.)
Oriental Moonstone (pearly)
Spinel varieties
Spinel Ruby
Pleonaste
Garnet Pyrope
Zircon varieties
Jargoon (white and yellow)
Hyacinth (brown and red)
Quartz varieties
Rock Crystal (colorless)
Amethyst (purple)
Cairngorm (smoky)
Chalcedony varieties
Carnelian (red and yellow)
Jasper varieties: black (Lydian stone), red and brown
Rutile (in quartz pebbles)
Topaz (white)
Magnetite
Titanic Iron
Magnesite
Tourmaline
Hornblende

The report emphasizes the facts that "the field is a large one, that the extent of sapphire wash is second to none in the world, and that a constant supply of stones could be maintained." It seems that these Australian gems have not met with the fair treatment so necessary in the development of the fields, and in their report Messrs. Rands and Dunstan submit an extract from a letter received from an important firm of lapidaries and gem merchants in Geneva: "Fine sapphires equal to those from Burma have been found amongst the Australian gem stones. Most of these are sent to Germany by dealers where they are sorted. The best gems are afterwards sold separately under another name, and the inferior lots sold as Australian."

Large sapphires are more frequently found than large rubies. Dr. Chambers mentions one discovered in 1853, in the alluvium a few miles from Ratnapoora, which was valued at over 4,000 pounds sterling. A large specimen, three inches long, is mentioned by Professor J. D. Dana as being in the possession of Sir Abram Hume. In the Green Vaults at Dresden several great specimens are shown. The large "Saphir merveilleux" which Mr. Hope exhibited at the London Exhibition in 1851, known as the "Hope Sapphire," was blue by daylight and amethyst by nightlight. This gem was last said to be in the Russian Treasury. (This sapphire has nothing in common with the blue cobalt-colored artificial spinels known as "Hope Sapphires.") Dr. G. F. H. Smith mentions several large stones, the most notable being one of 950 carats which was reported to be in the King of Ava's treasury in 1827. The weight of the Rospoli rough sapphire in the Jardin des Plantes is 132 carats. The Duke of Devonshire has a fine sapphire of 100 carats, brilliant cut above the girdle of the stone, and step cut below.

From the earliest times, the sapphire had the reputation of a holy gem. Solinus says that "it feels the air and sympathizes with the heavens, shining not the same if the sky be bright or obscured." The ancients held the gem sacred to Phoebus, not as a personification of the Sun, but rather, as explained by Dr. Alexander S. Murray (Department of Greek and Roman Antiquities in the British Museum), as follows:

"From the sun comes our physical light, but that light is at the same time an emblem of mental illumination, of knowledge, truth and right, of all moral purity. In this respect a distinction was made between it as a mental and a physical phenomenon—a distinction which placed Phoebus Apollo on one side and Helios on the other. Accordingly Phoebus Apollo is the oracular god who throws light on the dark ways of the future, who slays the Python—that monster of darkness which made the oracle at Delphi inaccessible. He is the god of music and song which are only heard where light and security reign and the possession of herds is free from danger." This is the ideal of the sign Aquarius, astrologically considered, and students of the old science well know that Solinus implies when he says that the gem of sign Aquarius "feels the air and sympathizes with the heavens" for this sign of "air," of fine ethereal forces, of "outer airs," of fine subtle substances, is also the sign of Heaven and the Heavens.

The great physician Galen used the sapphire "for expelling the hot humours of the body," which unfavorable health condition is included in astrological philosophy on the evils of the sign Aquarius. The sign also, as the astrologer Raphael says, "has particular rule over the eyesight, and the Sun conjoined with Saturn therein is a sure sign of blindness." Ancient writers say that he who gazes into a sapphire will charm away all threatened injury to his eyes, and Marbodus recommends that a sapphire "dissolved in milk" takes the sting from "dimmed eyes." For removing foreign bodies from the eye, specks of dust or sand, it was recommended that a sapphire be held a while on the closed eyelid and then drawn gently and slowly several times across from the nose to the corner of the eye.

It is one of the principles in medicine, astrologically administered, that the cause of the disease can also be used as a cure, while another rule advises the virtue of opposites. In this latter connection, it was said that a sapphire placed near the heart would fortify that organ, since the sign of Heaven ruling the heart is Leo, and Aquarius is exactly opposite to Leo in the zodiac. In homeopathic medicine, aconite in proper proportion is administered to reduce fevers and inflamed conditions. Astrologically, aconite is an herb of Saturn. Saturn is, like the herb, cold and contracting, while Mars is warm and expanding. The blood and mental faculties are liable to disorder in certain people born with Aquarius rising at birth or with the Sun therein. The sapphire was the panacea which also, it was said, stopped bleeding of the nose if held against the temples.

In old pharmacies, the sapphire held a place of importance and its reputed curative value led to its employment as a charm against swellings, boils, ruptures, profuse perspirations, poisons, melancholy, flatulence, and other bodily inharmonies. It was also employed as a charm against enchantment, danger, treachery, quarrels between friends, evil suggestions, and undue influence. Porta, in his work on *Natural Magic* (1561), writes of the value of the sapphire in all magical and religious ceremonies, protecting the wearer from the larvae of the lower spiritual world and from the snakes and poisonous reptiles of the world of matter. It was considered intensely powerful as a destroyer of poisonous insects, which it was said to kill if placed at the mouth of a vessel in which they were imprisoned.

Boetius (*De Natura Gemmarum*) writes that the sapphire was worn by priests as an emblem of chastity, for none of evil thoughts, bad minds, or vicious habits dare wear this gem of pure heavenly love which was used of old by those consulting the sacred oracles. In his messages to the Bishops of the 12th century, Pope Innocent III asked that they should have their pure gold rings set with "that stone which is the true seal of secrecy." When the Roman Catholic church received her novices into the Sisterhood a sapphire ring blessed by a Bishop was given as a holy symbol of the mystical marriage. In the famous Pulsky Collection, mentioned by Mr. C. W. King, there is a wonderful intaglio on a fine sapphire of Pope Paul III by the great Alessandro Cesati, three-quarters of an inch square. St. Jerome (4th and 5th centuries) wrote that the sapphire saved its wearer from captivity and pacified his enemies, and that it gained the favor of princes.

Some old authors recommend the sapphire as a stone for the hands of kings. It is a stone rather of democracy. Perhaps, however, the symbolic idea was that the king as a service to the people could adorn his hand with no more fitting emblem. It is traditionally reported that the ring of King Solomon was a sapphire, which stone was believed by some of the masters to be the special talisman of the Jews. One kept in the Holy of Holies as a holy emblem is said to have been saved and concealed for the people of Israel when Titus sacked Jerusalem. Moses was born with the Sun rising in the ascending Aquarius, hence the adoption of either the sapphire, as we know it today, or the lapis lazuli as national gems is perfectly natural.

The sapphire in the signet of Constantine, weighing 53 carats, which now lies amongst the treasures in the Rinuccini Cabinet at Florence, is cut in intaglio with a portrait of the Emperor in the guise of Nimrod attacking a great boar with his spear in the Caesarean plains. As a gem of heavenly and beautiful thoughts, the sapphire was regarded as a charm against devils, evil forces, witchcraft, sorcery, and all forms of villainy. The Buddhists symbolically say that a sapphire opens a closed door, brings prayerful feelings, and sounds the sweet bells of peace. It is a stone of truth, constancy, friendship, goodness, and angelic help; it warns against hidden dangers and heightens the imagination and psychic forces. It rebels against intoxication and refuses to adorn the hand of a drunkard; it helps hopes and wishes that are truly just and right. It was the third stone of the Nao-rattan and the fourth of the seven rings which Iarchus brought down from the angelic spheres as a gift to Apollonius of Tyana. It was the fourth stone of the magical necklace of Vishnu, and according to the Ramayana sapphires fell from the eyes of the slain god Maha Bali.

An Irish countess lent, for exhibition to the South Kensington Loan Collection in 1872, the sapphire ring which Lady Scroope threw from the window of the death chamber of Queen Elizabeth to Sir Robert Carey who was waiting below. This was the signal of the Queen's passing, and, Carey conveyed the news post haste to James.

In the Sepher of Solomon "which was set together in the desert by Children of Israel in the Holy Name of God, following the influences of the stars," a charm for favoring desires, for procuring invisibility, and certain benefits was a light-colored sapphire on which was engraved a mermaid holding a twig in one hand and a mirror in the other. The times for the construction of this talisman (which was to be set in a ring and worn inwards for escaping the eyes of others) was when the moon, well aspected, was passing through the 5th, 6th, and 7th degrees of the sign Aquarius. Another charm from the same source is the figure of a young man crowned, a circle round his neck, his hands raised in prayer, seated on a four-legged throne supported on the back of their necks by four men standing. The charm is to be cut on a "cornflower" sapphire for purifying the mind and obtaining favours from rulers, scholars, priests and people of wisdom, when the well-aspected moon was passing through the 1st, 2nd,

28th, and 29th degrees of Aquarius.

In the *Book of Wings*, a charm advised for gaining wealth and prophetic foresight is an astrolabe cut on a sapphire, especially when the moon, well aspected, passes through the 1st, 2nd, 28th, and 29th degrees of Aquarius. Another for health, protection from poison, poisonous airs, and tyranny was the bearded head of man or a ram engraved on a sapphire, constructed when the well-aspected moon was passing through 8th, 9th, 25th, and 26th degrees of Aquarius.

The asteriated or star sapphire, displaying like the star ruby, an opalescent star, is a valued charm for procuring the love of friends, for constancy and harmony. Dreaming of sapphires is said to denote protection, social success, and favor generally.

All shades of blue and green sapphires are under the zodiacal Aquarius. White sapphires (called Leucos sapphires) are under the sign Pisces. Yellow sapphires are under the sign Leo. Amethyst sapphires are under the sign Sagittarius.

CHAPTER XII

SARDONYX-SUCCINITE

Sardonyx: Schorl: Selenite: Comparisons By Marbodus and Malpleat. Pliny's Account: Ancient Use of Selenite: Used in the Palace at Pekin: Dr. John Goad and the Selenite of Pope Clement VIII: Selenite Amongst the Greeks: Trevisa's Narrative: Selenites or Lunary Men: A Love Attractor: A Curious Talisman: Selenite and Pearls: Serpentine or Hydrinus: Identified with the Tarshish Stone: The Ophite Stone of Dioscorides and Pliny: Agricola Knows it as Lapis Serpentius: The Ranochia of Italian Artists: A Cure for Rheumatic Affections: Used by the Ancients for Fashioning Ornaments and Charms: A Talisman of Capricorn: Used in the Making of Scarabs and Cylinders: Soapstone or Steatite: Its Extensive Use in Ancient Egypt: Pinite: The Agalmatolite or Pagodite Called by the Chinese Hao-Chi: Lucky Figures and Emblems: A Savage Food: Sphene or Titanite Spinel or Balas Ruby: Varieties: Phenomena of the Spinel: Albertus Magnus: Andrea Bacci: The Palace of the Ruby: Marco Polo's Story: Lal Rumani of the Indians: The King of Oude's Specimen: The Lal-i-Jaladi: The Black Prince's Ruby and Its Story: Sir James Melville and Queen Elizabeth's "Fair, Great Ruby": Love of Queen Elizabeth for Spinels: Robert De Berquen at the Court of the King of Persia: Spinels and Corundums in River Gravels; Elianus and the Story of the Stork; Its Symbolic Import: An Ancient Medical Custom: A Health Stone: A Garden Charm: Spodumene: Hiddenite: Kunzite: Radium Influence on Spodumene and Kunzite: Succinite.

SARDONYX: (see Onyx)

SCHORL: (see Tourmaline)

SELENITE:

> "This stone, a remedy for human ills,
>   Springs, as they tell, from famous Persia's hills."
> Marbodus

The word "selenite" is derived from the Greek selene, the moon, and is found also written as silenite, silonite, and silenitis. The stone which is a crystallized variety of gypsum is in pearly white, green, yellow, and gray colors. Marbodus compares it with soft grass or verdant jasper, and Malpleat, in 1567, says it is like a fresh and flourishing green herb. The moon-like lusters whether in pearl-white or light green are the most esteemed. Pliny writes that it is frequently employed in the construction of beehives to enable the curious to watch the little insects at their wonderful work.

The ancients employed it in much the same way as we do glass, and it formed an item of considerable trade importance between Rome, Spain, Cyprus, Africa, Cappodocia, and other parts of the ancient world. Slightly coarser varieties were used by Tiberius to cover his hot-houses, for it is susceptible of being split into comparatively thin sheets. A finer variety of very great value was at one time to be seen in the palace at Pekin. Dr. John Goad, who wrote the *Astro-Meteorologia*, a book on the natures and influences of the celestial bodies, mentions the selenite which Pope Clement VIII had amongst his treasures. It was a natural moon dial, of which Cocheram said in 1623, "it decreaseth and encreaseth as the moon groweth." This Dr. Goad was a famous scholar who, wrote Cooper, "gained a reputation for his astrological knowledge founded on reason and experiment."

The Greeks called the stone selenitis lithos, because they said it waxed and waned with the moon, a belief quaintly expressed by Trevisa in 1398 as follows: "Selenites is a stone of Perse, grene as grasse. It shineth with a white specke and foloweth the moon and waxyth and waneth as the moon doeth." Some old stories tell of a belief that little Moon men which Howell, a 17th century writer, calls "Selenites or Lunary Men," flung these stones deep in the earth.

The selenite was regarded as a love attractor and a stone to restore harmony between quarrelsome lovers. If engraved with a figure of Diana with bow and arrow, when the moon was passing through the 3rd, 16th, and 17th degrees of Cancer, it increased, say old writers, the power of imagination and helped the wearer to realize future movements. If the selenite be burned and carefully powdered, it is said to be of great use in cleaning pearls (which also are moon-ruled, according to astrology). The selenite is under the sign Cancer, like the moonstone with which it is frequently confounded.

SERPENTINE or **HYDRINUS:** The name serpentine appears at different periods as serpentyn, serpentyne, sarpentene, sarpentin, and scharpentyn. It is derived from the Latin serpens, and its more ancient term hydrinus indicates exactly the sea serpent family (hydridae) so well known to ancient and modern writers. Precious serpentine is translucent, or nearly so, and of a rich oily green color. Common serpentine is opaque. The precious serpentine is called "noble," the impure "common." The colors are dark oily green, light green, olive green, black green, brown yellow, green yellow, and sometimes almost white.

The serpentine is identified with the Tarshish stone, the tenth stone of the High Priest's Breastplate. It was known as "ophite stone" by Dioscorides and Pliny, and Agricola, writing in the16th century, calls it "lapis serpentinus." Other writers called it "serpentinum," hence the modern name "serpentine." In Italy, especially amongst artists, some specimens of the stone are known as "ranochia," because of its similarity to a frog's skin.

It was recommended of old as a cure for rheumatism and rheumatic pains in the limbs, and for that purpose specimens were carried on the body next to the skin, attached to the arms or legs. It was believed to cure dropsy and all moist complaints, especially if the sufferer held a specimen in each hand while resting in the sunlight. The wearer was also warned not to overdo this sun-bathing with serpentine in his hands because of its affinity with all natural bodily fluids. It was said to be a charm against serpent bites or stings and to scare away poisonous insects and reptiles of the sea and land. Serpentine was much esteemed by the ancients for its healing virtues and peculiar beauty. They effectively employed it in the manufacture of vases, pillars, and boxes for the making of special charms and talismans. The figure of a goat with a fish's tail cut on a serpentine when the moon, well aspected, was passing through the 3rd and 4th degrees of the sign Capricorn, was a charm against rheumatism, skin troubles, gout, stiff limbs, accidents to the limbs, falls, or hurts.

The serpentine was largely used by the ancient Egyptians in the making of sacred scarabs, and the Persians favored it especially for shaping into cylinders of authority, one of which is described by Mr. C. W. King as follows:

"A King contending with two andro-sphinxes, Ormuzd
hovering above on the Tree of Life"—a very symbolic cylinder.
The serpentine or hydrinus is under the celestial Capricorn.

SOAPSTONE or **STEATITE:** Steatite derives its name from the Greek word stear, fat, which well describes the greasy feel of this soft magnesian rock, a massive variety of talc. It was extensively used by the ancient Egyptians, who cut it into scarabs which, in many cases, they first burned and then coated with a vitreous blue or green glaze. The substance is extremely soft and can easily be cut with a knife. Soapstone figures are cut from a variety known as pinite, the agalmatolite or pagodite which the Chinese called Hoa-chi. Many of these are very beautifully cut, a number being lucky figures in the guise of gods and goddesses, flowers, and fruits. This custom reminds one of the "household gods" of the ancients. A kind of soft steatite earth is still eaten by the savages of New Caledonia and other places. All varieties of steatite are under the zodiacal Taurus.

SPHENE or **TITANITE:** Sphene derives its name from the Greek sphen, a wedge. As the name indicates the form of the crystals is wedge-shaped. The luster is very brilliant, but the stone is scarcely as hard as the opal and therefore is little used in jewelry. Sphene is under the zodiacal Sagittarius.

SPINEL or **BALAS RUBY:** Spinel, which derives its name from the Greek word spinos, a spark, is found written in a variety of ways, chief amongst which are spinell, spinele, and spinel. Its colors are red, brown, green, yellow, and blue. The red varieties are clear and glittering and the dark generally more dense or opaque.

The name spinel is applied to those of bright red color.
The name balas is applied to those of rose red.
The name rubicelle is applied to those of orange red.
The name almandine is applied to those of violet.
The name chloro spinel is applied to those of green.
The name ceylonite or pleonaste is applied to those of black.
The name sapphirine is applied to those of blue.

Spinel and Balas are often intermixed, and both terms are accepted as denoting this aluminate of magnesium, whose hardness is just a little inferior to the corundum and whose crystalline form is isometric, like the diamond. The spinel, however, is non-electric, no matter if submitted to heat or friction, while the ruby (corundum) and garnet are highly so. Hence, it is not a difficult matter to distinguish these stones from each other, even if their outward similarities tend to confuse the eye. The spinel, submitted to trial by heat, first changes from red to brown; if left to cool it becomes dark; then it changes to green; then, as if exhausted, it seems to lose its color which, however, slowly reappears in its red expression.

The word balas has been written as balace, baless, balays, balais, and balass. It is derived from the Arabic balakhsh which, says Albertus Magnus, is the female of the real ruby "and some say it is his house." That prolific writer on precious stones, Andrea Bacci (16th and 17th centuries), echoes older thought also when he writes that "Balas is derived from Palatius, a palace, which is the palace where the ruby lives." He echoes the symbolic ideas of the old Greek writers who said that the true ruby resided in a palace, clearly showing that they knew the difference between rubies and spinels. Marco Polo's remarks are as follows: "In this Provence (Badachschan), those fine and valuable gems the Balas rubies are found. They are got in certain rocks among the mountains and in the search for them the people dig great caves beneath the earth just as is done by miners for silver. There is but one special mountain that produces them and it is called Syghinan. The stones are dug on the King's account and no one else dares dig on pain of death as well as of seizure of worldly possession, nor may any take the gems out of the Kingdom. The King collects them all and sends them to other kings as tribute or as presents. He so acts in order to keep the Balas at a great value for if he allowed all persons to mine for them the world would be filled with them and they would be valueless."

In Persia there is a story which tells that they were found in a destroyed mountain after an earthquake. The Indians know the stone as the "Pomegranate Ruby" (Lal Rumani), and the King of Oude is said to have had a remarkable and beautiful specimen as big as the egg of a pigeon, which was known as "Lal-i-jaladi." The beautiful heart-shaped balas which is set in the British Crown under the Black Cross known as the "Black Prince's Ruby," is said to have been obtained in Spain by Prince Edward when he was aiding Don Pedro of Castillo to hold his throne. It is reported that this was the gem worn by King Henry V at the Battle of Agincourt. This may have been the "fair great ruby" which Sir James Melville says Queen Elizabeth valued so highly. Elizabeth was very fond of spinels of which she possessed some splendid specimens, as shown in the still extant inventories of the personal effects of the Queen. An inspection of her nativity will show that they were gems of good omen for her.

Madame de Barrera gives an extract from Robert de Berquen's *Merveilles des Indes Orientales et Occidentales* wherein it is stated that "Josephus Barbaro, a Venetian gentleman, says in a report made to the Signori of Venice that when he was ambassador for the Republic at the court of Yussum Cassan, King of Persia, on a certain day of the year 1472 when he was received in solemn audience, that prince showed him a handkerchief filled with the rarest and most inestimable precious stones. Among others there was a table-cut Balass ruby, of a beautiful shape, of at least a finger's breadth, weighing two ounces and a half, and of a most peerless colour: in fact, it was a most perfect paragon, so exquisite that when the king asked what he valued it at, he replied that he thought a city or even a kingdom would scarcely pay for it."

Spinels and corundum are always found together, and Dr. G. F. H. Smith comments on the fact that, although they are harder stones, rubies in river gravels are usually waterworn, while spinels are found in perfect crystals. The ancient zoologist Elianus repeats an old story that a stork brought a spinel as a present to the woman-nurse Heraclis for healing his wounded leg. Here again it is necessary to look beneath the fable for true understanding of it. The stork is one of the birds of Jupiter, and its legs are astrologically under the zodiacal Sagittarius (the house or mansion of Jupiter). The woman symbolizes the moon, and in her name the afternoon sun is concealed. The nurse is under Virgo, the sign to which the spinel is attached. The four toes of the stork symbolize the negative or afternoon sun, the three front toes webbed to the first joint, Jupiter. Again, the stork has no voice and tells no secrets. Hence we have a cryptic prescription illustrating the method employed by the ancient medical brethren to convey their meaning to each other. The spinel is here an active mineral employed in the treatment, together with the moon and negative or afternoon sun, of certain afflications of the legs. Even today it is a custom amongst medical men to preface their prescriptions with the symbol of Jupiter. The stork is also greatly esteemed as a bird of good fortune and happy omen, and in many countries it is protected against destruction.

The spinel was esteemed as a perfect health stone and was especially valued as a charm to be worn over the solar plexus. It was a fortunate gem for doctors of medicine, scholars, writers, clerks, secretaries, manufacturers, business people, hospital attendants, and nurses. It raised the thoughts and purified the imagination. A specimen placed at each corner of a house was considered a protection against calamity, and rough pieces placed at the four angles of a garden, orchard, or corn field were said not only to protect the products from storms and lightning, but also to carry the symbolic influence of rich returns for the farmer.

The spinel or balas, rubicelle, almandine ruby, and the sapphirine are under the zodiacal Virgo. The chloro-spinel and the pleonaste are under the zodiacal Capricorn.

SPODUMENE: Spodumene derives its name from the Greek word spodios, ash-colored. It is a stone resembling feldspar, but has a luster more pearl-like. In general appearance, spodumene is of a pale yellow tint, sometimes gray, or as its name suggests, ash-colored. It is about the hardness of quartz. The emerald green variety which is exceedingly rare, is called hiddenite, after its discoverer, Mr. M. G. Hidden, and it is said by Professor Dana to rival the emerald as a gem. It was discovered in 1881 in North Carolina, which seems to be the only place of its occurrence. Comparatively, few specimens have been distributed and amongst them no stones of any considerable size. A pretty example of 2 1/2 carats is in the Natural History section of the British Museum.

Perhaps the most beautiful examples of this mineral were discovered in the San Diego district of California in 1903 and named kunzite, after Dr. G. F. Kunz. These stones range in color from pale violet to deep lilac, and large specimens have already been unearthed, the one in the British Museum weighing 60 carats. Dr. G. F. H. Smith remarks that under the influence of radium, kunzite is phosphorescent, thus presenting some difference from spodumene in general. In analysis it is shown that spodumene contains 7.5 percent of lithia. It would be, in harmony with ancient philosophy, under the zodiacal Libra, although the variety hiddenite may be connected with the zodiacal Taurus. All varieties of spodumene would be regarded as powerful eye charms and as beneficial to the kidneys and lumbar regions.

SUCCINITE: (see Garnet)

CHAPTER XIII

TITANITE-TOPAZ

Titanite: Topaz: The Mystery of the "Island of the Mists": The Ring of Thomas A' Becket Called a Peritot by the Abbot of Glastonbury: The Meaning of the Word Topaz: Topaz Remarkable for Its Cleavage: Its Use in Ancient and Modern Medicine: Topaz Rhombicus of the Mineralogists: M. Dumelle Discovers How to Change the Color of a Topaz: "Pingos D'Agoa," "Gouttes D'Eau," "Minas Novas": "Diamond of Slaves": Twelve Pounds of Topaz for Three Shillings: How Queen Mary's Great Blue Topaz Was Found: The Topazion Statue of Ptolemy Philadelphus: The Ptolemaic Badge: Hadrian's Topaz: Topaz of the Grand Mogul and Runyeet Singh: A Giant Emperor's Pleasure: Some Old Intagli: Pliny's Stone of Strength: A Stone Against Death and Terror: Symbol of Boiling Water: A Charm Against Drowning: A Modern Illustration: Rabbi Benoni: "Book of Winds": Topaz Charms.

TITANITE: (see Sphene)

TOPAZ:

"The flaming topaz with its golden beam."
Glover

At various times the word has been rendered tupase, tupace, topace, topas, thopas, topaze, topasie, topazius, and topasius. In the traditional derivation of the word, a mystery is concealed. Pliny says that the stone was found in an island difficult for mariners to locate on account of the fogs and mists surrounding it, and Marbodus seems to indicate the true topaz when he says:

"From seas remote the yellow topaz came,
Found in the island of the self-same name."

The island was known as Topazios, which owes its origin to the Greek word meaning "to divine, guess, conjecture." The misty island is the celestial Scorpio, which is accounted in astrophilosophy the death sign and the sign of the serpent, the wounder of the heel of man. It also concerns the goods of the departed, and their abode in the world to come. Hence the Island of the Mists is the place of guess, conjecture, or philosophical speculation which the traveler in the flesh can dimly see through the strange cloudy lights of the spirit. The name was originally given to the stone known to us as the chrysolite, which gem is now identified with the occult sign of the fishes employed in the mysteries in ancient and modern times.

The classification as we at present know it, is of very ancient date, and specimens of the modern topaz have been found adorned with various intaglios of proven antiquity. Although it has been stated that Thomas A' Becket wore a topaz ring, there is no doubt that Adam Sodbury, Abbot of Glastonbury, was correct when he says it was a peridot, for the peridot or chrysolite was the stone of the churchmen and intimately associated with the mystic sign of Christianity—Pisces, the Fishes. The old abbot wrote that "a gold ring in which was set the stone peritot (an old form of peridot) encircled the finger of our martyr St. Thomas when he was killed by the swords of evil men." At that time it is certain that the topaz and the peridot were the stones known as such today, and as such they had been known for many centuries before.

The Sanskrit word topas, meaning heat, may well describe the topaz, the color of which can be changed readily by heat, and which, under heat pressure, and friction, exhibits strong electric phenomena.

Scorpio, as before remarked, is the sign of the snake or serpent so intimately connected with the mysteries of life and death, and the topaz is remarkable for its cleavage, for when struck with a hammer it breaks into flakes like the backbone of a serpent. The topaz was considered as of wonderful potency in the treatment of sexual disorders, which astrologically are considered as disorders of the sign Scorpio. It contains from 55 to 58 percent of alumina, which substance has been used in modern times by Dr. Richard Hughes, Dr. Teste, Dr. Peters, Dr. Marcy, and others in troubles of the sexual system and the mucous membranes. The drug has been used homeopathically in such morbid conditions and in chronic pharyngitis and diseases of the nose and throat. The nose is ruled by Scorpio in astrological deductions, and the throat by Taurus, its opposite sign. Alumina is most strongly expressed in corundums, which include oriental topaz, chrysoberyl, spinel, and topaz. But there are certain characteristics of the topaz which in some way render it distinct from other gems, and these would have been considered by the hermetic schools whence such philosophy originated.

Amongst mineralogists, topaz is known as topaz rhombicus. It is found in colors golden, yellow, reddish, white, greenish, wine color, and blue. A charming pink is produced artificially by subjecting the real stone to heat, the best results being procured from a golden-brown variety. This process was first discovered by M. Dumelle, a Paris jeweler, in the year 1750. The color thus obtained is doubtless permanent, the shade being manifest when the stone cools. Great care must be observed in this simple experiment because the stone is so sensitive that, unless properly handled, it is likely to split under the various degrees of heat and cold.

Translucent achromatic topaz is called pingos d'agoa (drops of water) by the Brazilians, and gouttes d'eau by the French. In England the variety is called minas novas, after the Minas Novas in the State of Minas Geraes in Brazil where it is extensively found. In Portugal this type of topaz is called the "Diamond of Slaves." The large British Museum specimen of this white topaz which, according to Mr. Emanuel, weighs over 12 pounds (avoirdupois), was sold for three shillings by a marine store dealer who used it to hold open his door.

The great blue Queensland topaz, in the possession of Queen Mary of Great Britain, is said to have been discovered by a shepherd who, thinking it was a common stone, threw it at a howling dog during the night and wakened in the morning to discover the precious nature of his missile. The Topazion Statue of four cubits high, which Pliny mentions as having been made by the order of Ptolemy Philadelphus to the memory of his sister-wife Arsinoe, has puzzled investigators. It has been set down as indicating a statue of jasper, agate, prase, chrysoprase, or rock crystal of the citrine or smoky quartz varieties. Probably this latter suggestion is right, but the real meaning will no doubt lie in the sign Scorpio, which was known in old Egypt as the Eagle (the symbolic badge of the Ptolemaic dynasty) and was the sign of material death and spiritual life. The Emperor Hadrian is said to have had a large topaz ring on which was engraved:

"Natura deficit,
Fortuna mutatur,
Deus omnia cernit."

Tavernier writes of a great topaz in the possession of the Grand Mogul weighing 157 carats and worth about 100,000 dollars. Runyeet Singh's topaz, half the size of a billiard ball, was worth 200,000 rupees. The Great Braganza, 1680 carats, which adorned the crown of Portugal, and was supposed to be a diamond, is a white topaz. One of the pleasures of the giant Emperor Maximilian, of whose strength so many stories are told, was to crush topazes to powder in his fingers. Why he indulged in this form of sport is unknown; probably he found it recreation after killing an ox at a blow or knocking out the teeth of an unfortunate horse. Mr. King mentions a Head of Maecenas on topaz attributed to Solon at Florence, and another, wrongly attributed to Dioscorides, of a girl's head in the Marlborough collection.

The topaz was called "stone of strength" by Pliny for the martial Scorpio is the wrestler's sign and the sign of strong people. The power of the topaz was said to increase as the moon increased, especially if the night orb was at new or full in the sign Scorpio. It banished the terrors of the night, protected the wearer during epidemics, soothed the wild passions, and gave a glimpse of the beyond. It banished the fear of death and secured a painless passing from this life to the next; it gave strength to the intellect and enabled the wearer to receive impressions from astral sources. It preserved from miasmatic conditions and lost its color when in the presence of poisons. The power attributed to it of quenching boiling water is symbolic of the fiery Mars, planet of power in the watery Scorpio.

It was also said by the old masters that the topaz preserved against drowning, and a curious illustration of this belief came recently under the writer's notice. He advised the wife of a well-known Australian to purchase a very beautiful topaz, which was mounted under his direction as a charm of the sign Scorpio. During the late war this lady and her daughter had need to travel to England. The voyage was about half accomplished when the vessel was submarined. The boat in which the lady and her daughter were, capsized and all the struggling passengers were thrown into the sea. She seized a piece of wreckage and supported her daughter and herself until they were both dragged into a boat some considerable time after. The lady had clutched the topaz charm from her neck and was holding it tightly in her hand while struggling in the water. Just as they got into the boat, she felt someone give a heavy blow on her hand and take the gem from her. She grieved for the loss of her beautiful topaz charm which she regarded as the symbol of her own and her daughter's salvation.

Leonardus said that topaz was a charm against asthma, and Rabbi Benoni calls it the emblem of strength and the easer of hemmorhage. In the *Book of Wings*, it is recommended that to secure favor with kings, princes, nobles, and important personages a topaz engraved with the figure of a flying falcon should be worn. This charm was to be constructed as a charm of power when the well-aspected moon was passing through the 5th, 6th, and 7th degrees of the heavenly Scorpion. Another topaz charm given is for acquiring riches. This takes the form of a man holding a lamp. It had to be mounted in gold and constructed when the increasing moon, in good aspect to the direct Jupiter and the Sun, was passing through the 5th, 6th, 7th, 26th, and 27th degrees of Scorpio.

In a dream, the topaz is a symbol of movement and protection from harm, and poisons. The symbolic dream introducing this stone is a symbolic message from the departed. The topaz and its varieties are under the celestial Scorpio.

Topaz

CHAPTER XIV

TOURMALINE-ZIRCON

Tourmaline: Arrival of Specimens in London: The Ash Attractor: The "Electric Stone" of Linnaeus: The "Magnetic" of Lemery: Experiments of Aepinus and Lehmann: Professor Goodchild's Experiment: Suspected Connection of the Tourmaline with Oriental Alchemy: Colors of the Tourmaline: The Tourmaline and the Topaz in Methylene Iodide: Identification Suggestions: Pliny's Lychnis: The Caduceus of Hermes: Turquoise: Saxo and Albertus Magnus on Its Virtues: The Piruzeh of the Arabians: The Chalchihuitl of the Mexicans: Identified with Pliny's Callais: A Favorite Oriental Charm Stone: A Symbolic Theory of Origin: Stone of the Horse and Rider: A Religious Gem of Jupiter: A Charm Against the Evil Eye: A Sensitive Stone: Mistakes of Writers: Medicinal Values: Turquoise Set in Statues of Buddha: The Golden Bow and Turquoise Arrow: Gem of the Gods: Color Changes in Turquoise: Turquoise and the Weather: Indian Rain Stone: King Toheser and the Turquoise Mines: Major C. MacDonald and Professor Flinders Petrie Discover the Old Turquoise Workings: Love of the Turquoise in Old Egypt: Some Unique Stones: The Gem in Persia: The Khorassan Mines: Stone of Fashion in 17th Century Europe: Death Stone of James IV of Scotland: Henry VIII Sends a Last Gift to Cardinal Wolsey: Marbodus's Turquoise Talisman of Freedom: Difference Between "De Vielle Roche" and "De Nouvelle Roche": Variscite: Identified as the Callaina of Pliny: Mane er H'Rock or Fairy Rock of Brittany: Zircon: Stone of the Moon's Nodes: The Snakes of the Caduceus.

TOURMALINE:

"This black thing, one of the prettiest of the very few pretty black things in the world, is called Tourmaline."

Ruskin

The tourmaline, written in the 18th century in England as tumalin, is derived from the Ceylonese turmali or toramalli. The first specimens to arrive in London were known as "Brazilian emeralds," and they came from Brazil in the 17th century only to meet with an unfavorable reception. In the beginning of the 18th century Dutch merchants began to bring from Amsterdam specimens obtained by them from Ceylon. The Dutch cutters, observing how straw and other particles were attracted to specimens which had been lying in the sunlight, called the stone aschentrekker (ash attractor). The Germans called it azchenzieher, and the French tire-cendre.

The Swedish scholar Linnaeus experimented with the tourmaline, calling it the "electric stone." M. Lemery, the French Professor, called it the "magnetic." The experiments of Aepinus and Lehmann were concerned with the positive and negative energies exhibited by tourmaline. These 18th century scholars held that its power of repulsion exceeded its power of attraction. This sensitive stone is affected by weather changes, and it exhibits considerable power when heated, the electricity then developed being termed pyro-electric. Professor W. Goodchild, M.B., details an interesting experiment in dealing with the physical properties of gem stones.

"A crystal of tourmaline, in heating to 150 degrees C, becomes positively electrified at one terminature and negatively at the other. If now it be suspended by a non-conducting thread it will act as a magnet. On cooling, the charges on the poles reverse, positive becoming negative. If a crystal with such a charge be dusted with a fine mixture of sulphur and red lead, the yellow sulphur will be attracted to the portions charged with positive electricity, while the red lead goes to the negatively charged portions."

This experiment serves to illustrate the attraction of the mind (represented by yellow sulphur), towards the positive pole, and matter (represented by red lead), towards the negative pole, as noted in the philosophical researches of the old alchemists. If in a heated state the tourmaline be shattered, all the little pieces will exhibit the forces of attraction and repulsion so marked in this strange stone. It has been suspected, not without reason, that tourmaline specimens were used by some of the Eastern students of alchemy who held primarily that the substance of the Philosopher's Stone is mercurial and that it should be treated with heat, for by that means alone would its use be shown, warmth coming from the Heavens to bless Man, Nature and the Kingdoms of Nature.

The tourmaline is also remarkable for the variety of its colors, indicated by various and not always appropriate names. Schorl, the black variety spoken of by Ruskin, was so called, according to De Costa (1761), by the German miners. The same writer says "our English miners call them 'bockle' and 'ball'." The name appears as shirl, schirl (so spelled by

De Costa), schoerl, and shorl. In the 16th century it was known in Germany as Schrul, but later in the 18th century appears as schorl. The name is now becoming unpopular, the simple term black tourmaline being preferred. The colorless variety is termed achroite, from a Greek word meaning colorless; pink and rosy red are termed rubellite; indigo blue, indicolite; blue, Brazilian sapphire; green, Brazilian emerald; yellow-green, Brazilian peridot; honey-yellow, Ceylon peridot; red violet, siberite. The brown variety is usually known as brown tourmaline, although it is sometimes called Brazilian topaz or Ceylonese topaz. It is not so hard as the topaz, however, ranging in the scale somewhere between quartz and zircon. The refractive powers are likewise not in agreement, and in methylene dioxide the topaz (stone of Mars) sinks, while the tourmaline (stone of Mercury) floats. There are also amber-colored, cinnamon, lilac, gray, blue-gray, water-green, and many beautiful parti-colored specimens.

It is believed by some students that this gem was known to the ancients by the name lyncurium, which Mr. King believes to be a species of jacinth, Dr. Brotero an orange-colored hyacinth. Professor Ajasson, believing the name to refer to tourmaline, suggests that lyn may be derived from the Sanskrit word Lanka, the name of Ceylon, a place where the stone is plentifully found. The general opinion now is that the stone described by Pliny under the name of lychnis is our tourmaline. Pliny writes, in his 37th Book on Natural History, of the power of the lychnis of drawing straws and fluff towards it when heated by the sun or by the friction of the hand.

The peculiar attractive and repulsive properties of the tourmaline may be compared with the mysteries contained in the caduceus of the wise and ever-restless Hermes. The symbolical snakes which adorn the rod represent knowledge received and knowledge imparted in the hermetic scheme of the Rosicrucians. The tourmaline is symbolical of wisdom, strength of mind, eloquence, learning, and the power of knowledge. It is the stone for the author, poet, editor, and teacher. To dream of it means, in harmony with ancient philosophy, success through knowledge in all walks of life. The tourmaline in all colors is under the zodiacal Gemini.

TURQUOISE:

"The fair Queen of France
 Sent him a turquoise ring and glove,
 And charged him as her knight and love
 For her to break a lance."
Sir Walter Scott

Turquoise has been written in a remarkable number of ways, amongst them being turky, torkey, turquay, turkey stone, turkie, turkeis, turkese, turkise, turkes, turkas, turkis (as used by Tennyson), turkoise, turkez, turqueis, turques, turchis, turquesse, torchas, turcasse, turquez, toorkes, and turkesse. The Venetians call it turchesa, the French turquoise, and the Germans turkis. Andrea Bacci (*De Gemmis et Lapidibus Pretiosis,* 1605) says that this stone is called turcicus, "Either on account of its admirable loveliness or for the reason that it is obtained from the Turks."

The name as we have it does not seem to go further back than the 13th century when Saxo, agreeing with Albertus Magnus, writes of it and praises its virtues as a preventive of accidents to the eye. The old Persians called it Piruzeh, the Triumphant, and the Arabians, whose special luck stone the turquoise is, engrave on specimens the name of Allah with a verse from the Koran or with some magical sign inserted in pure gold. It is known to the Mexicans as chalchihuitl. This stone is identified with the callais of Pliny, who relates symbolically that it was shot down by means of slings from unapproachable rock lands. The symbol has relation to the power of this stone of the Heavenly Archer over seemingly terrifying obstacles when firmly directed by the compelling will.

The turquoise is favored by Eastern occult students, who employ it largely in the composition of amulets and charms. It was said to have sprung up like an eye from its matrix, and is identified with the Antares in the Archer of the Heavens. These stars were indicated as affecting the eyes in the same degree as the Pleiades and the Asselli of Taurus and Leo. In modern Egypt, a turquoise is applied to the eye as a remedy for cataract and other ophthalmic troubles, specimens thus employed being usually engraved with the sacred name of Allah.

The turquoise is especially the stone of horses, mules, and camels, and from most ancient times specimens have adorned their trappings. Leonardus said that so long as a horseman carried a piece of turquoise with him while riding he would never have an accident, nor would his horse be fatigued, for it was believed that the stone would draw the pain of the accident to itself. Boetius de Boodt says that when riding to his house along an uncertain road on a dark night he fell with his horse down a declivity, but neither he nor his animal suffered hurt. His turquoise, however, was shattered. The stone was carried by jockeys, huntsmen, and horsemen generally as a symbol of the special protection of Jupiter.

In the Middle Ages, the turquoise was much worn by young girls who regarded it as a religious jewel for the protection of their virtue and for the uplifting of their thoughts. In the most ancient science, the sign Sagittarius, the house or mansion of the plant Jupiter, is the sign of sport, horses, dreams, high philosophy, religion (not in the sense of creed), the true lamp of life, long voyages, and publications (not newspapers). Thus the turquoise, as the stone of Sagittarius, was a stone of dreams, the horse, philosophy, and religion. Its grand symbolic purpose was to help the spiritual person to resist the weakness, evils, and temptations so intermixed with material life. The turquoise was said to be a charm against the evil eye and evil thoughts.

The Arabs say that the stone is sensitive to weather changes and that its color is affected by the state of the atmosphere. They knew Jupiter as the "Cloud Gatherer," "The Thunderer," and "The God of the Murky Cloud," and they connected turquoise with his powerful works. The planet Jupiter strong at birth is held to indicate riches and worldly advantage. The old Arabian writers note a form of magic for inducing wealth and monetary advantages, performed in the hour of Jupiter. During this ceremony, a turquoise was held in the right hand and the desires spoken into the stone at which a steady gaze was directed.

Carelessness has led to error amongst writers. A 16th century author confuses the topaz with the turquoise, describing the latter as a "gem of yellow color" and recommending it as a charm against bites of reptiles and stings of insects, qualities ascribed by the old masters to the topaz, gem of the sign of the Scorpion. Another writer repeats the error, saying that "this yellow stone reduced to a powder is helpful in case of stings from scorpions and fearful and venomous reptiles." The turquoise was held in esteem for diseases of the hip, a part of the body astrologically under the sway of Sagittarius. In this connection the stone was reduced to a paste and bound flat to the part affected, whole specimens being bound above and below the seat of the trouble.

The turquoise contains a high percentage of phosphoric acid, which is employed in modern homeopathy for affections of the lungs, astrologically under the sign Gemini and therefore opposite to the sign Sagittarius. The ancients advised the turquoise as a lung medicine, not to be taken internally.

The turquoise was also recommended for diseases of the throat and heart as phosphoric acid is today in homeopathy. The sign Sagittarius is also the sign of prophecy, and the turquoise set in the foreheads of the statues of Buddha and other images symbolizes the knowledge of things to come. The golden bow and the turquoise arrow of the Tibetan legend has special reference to the Sun in the sign Sagittarius. Dr. Kunz, quoting from Dr. Berthold Laufer of the Field Museum, Chicago, refers to this legend as follows:

"A powerful saint touching the bow and arrow of a blacksmith transforms the bow into gold and the arrow into turquoise." The bow represents the solar rays and the arrow the Heavens, hence it is little wonder that the turquoise was termed the "gem of the Gods." In harmony with an ancient astrophilosophy known as "Planetary Interchanges," the turquoise was considered an ideal lover's gift, unless the stone was otherwise than fortunate in the horoscope of the recipient, and a gift of friendship.

The changes of color in a turquoise have been long noted, and the lines of the poet Donne are frequently quoted:

"As a compassionate turquoise that doth tell
 By looking pale the wearer is not well."

Boetius tells a story of a wonderful turquoise possessed by a Spanish gentleman which so lost its color after his death that it appeared "more like a malachite than a turkois." Boetius then says that his father bought it for very little at the sale of the Spaniard's effects and gave it to him. He relates that he had hardly worn it for a month when "it resumed its pristine beauty and daily appeared to increase in splendour." Mr. Harry Emanuel gives a somewhat similar story concerning a turquoise that lost its luster with the death of its owner "as if mourning for its master," regaining it in its "former exquisite freshness" when worn by its new owner. A case of this kind came under the writer's notice. The wife of a well-known pastoralist of New South Wales had a bangle of turquoises cut into the shape of Egyptian scarabs. While traveling in Japan, she became ill, and the stones changed from a soft blue to a dull green, regaining their former beauty when the lady regained her health. One of the oldest firms of jewelers in the city of Melbourne, Australia, was worried to find that an exquisite Persian turquoise entrusted to them to mount in a tiara with diamonds was changing color while in the hands of their chief "setter." This craftsman had been complaining for some days of indisposition. The gem regained its beautiful color on being entrusted to another and healthier workman.

The connection of the turquoise with weather changes is not confined merely to Oriental peoples. The Pueblo and Apache Indians employ it as a rainstone, which they say is always found concealed at the foot of the rainbow. They also place pieces of turquoise on their bows and fire arms as directing charms for trueness of aim.

This stone is also called the "gem of liberty and benevolence," and an old Eastern proverb says, "A turquoise given with the hand of love carries with it true fortune and sweet happiness." Another Eastern belief runs that the turquoise turns pale when danger threatens the giver. Felton in his *Secrete Wonders of Nature*, 1569, states that "the turkeys does move when there is any peril prepared to him that weareth it." Dr. E. A. Wallis Budge identifies Tscheser of the 3rd dynasty (3900 B.C.) who built the "Step Pyramid" at Sakkarah as the Memphian King who worked the turquoise mines of Sinai. His name is still perpetuated on a rock at Wadi Magharah. It was at this place that Major C. MacDonald found turquoise in 1849, and Professor Flinders Petrie in 1905. Professor Petrie also discovered evidences here of very ancient mining operations.

Archaic specimens of worked turquoise are still being found in Egypt. The color appealed to the sons and daughters of Khem who imitated it to a very great extent in their scarabs, beads, ornaments, and other articles of adornment. In the Vatican collection there are valuable intaglios and cameos cut in this stone, which in some instances retain their heaven-blue color to this day. Mr. King mentions a laureated head of Augustus and the Head of a Gorgon in the Fould collection, "the original azure converted into a dull green by the action of the earth." In Persia the stone was always highly esteemed, and the most perfect specimens are held by the Royal House. The Khorassan mines near Nishapur are still famous for the remarkable beauty of the stones won from them.

So fashionable was the gem in Europe in the 17th century that no true gentleman would consider his dress complete unless his hand was adorned with a ring of turquoise, for it was (as a true stone of the Archer) symbolic of the fairness and high sense of justice of the wearer. The famous turquoises in the Royal Jewels of Spain were brought from New Mexico somewhere about this period. Sir Walter Scott in *Marmion* sings of the turquoise ring and glove which the French Queen sent to the Scottish King James IV, with 14,000 crowns of France, begging him for the love she had for him to raise an army for her sake. It is a curious fact that the turquoise was the death stone of James IV who was killed at Flodden Field by an arrow from an archer's bow. The turquoise was to him a symbol of error and fatality.

Henry VIII sent the dying Cardinal Wolsey a ring of turquoise by Sir John Russel, bidding him say to his fallen favorite that he, the king, "loved him as well as ever he did and grieved for his illness." For a talisman of liberty and freedom, Marbodus advises that a perfect turquoise be engraved with a man standing under a beetle. It should be then set in a brooch of gold and blessed and consecrated; "then the glory which God hath bestowed shall manifest." An astrological charm for wealth and prosperity takes the form of a centaur firing an arrow upwards, to be engraved on a turquoise, preferably in the hour of Jupiter with the Moon in good aspect to Jupiter passing the 3rd and 4th degrees of Sagittarius.

True turquoise, termed "de vieille roche," or oriental turquoise, differs from the fossil turquoise or odontolite, called "de nouvelle roche," or occidental turquoise. Fossil turquoise can be easily marked by a steel instrument, while true turquoise acts as flint to steel. A drop of hydrochloric acid causes effervescence in fossil turquoise, which when submitted to fire gives out an animal odor. Fine turquoises are of that heavenly blue color known as "turquoise blue," and they present a waxy appearance. The variety known as variscite, supposed to be the callaina of Pliny, is a soft green stone found in various forms in prehistoric graves near Mane er H'rock or Fairy Rock in Brittany, in the state of Utah in the United States of America, and other places. The turquoise is under the zodiacal Sagittarius.

ZIRCON: The name zircon is said to be derived from the Arabic zirk, a jewel. It was known in sanskrit as Rahuratna or stone of the Nodes of the Moon (Caput draconis and Caudadraconis), called the dragons of solar and lunar eclipses. These dragons were controlled by the magical power of Mercury and may also be compared to the snakes of the Caduceus. The Zircon is a transparent to opaque stone and has been noticed more fully under the names jargoon and hyacinth. The zircon is under the zodiacal Virgo.

CHAPTER XV

STONES IN SHAKESPEARE'S PLAYS

"It seems she hangs upon the cheek of night
Like a rich jewel in an Ethiope's ear."
Romeo and Juliet

Those who labor for the world belong to the world, no matter which little part of it may be claimed as their birthplace. This applies to the humblest as well as to the greatest, as in a play the excellence of individual players contributes to the artistic harmony and influence of the entire production. So it is that William Shakespeare, the inspired master of the "spacious times of great Elizabeth," breaks through the narrow limits of sea-girt England and encompasses the whole world of women and men, detaches his unmaterial self from the period of his earth life and endures, a perpetual source of pleasure, philosophy, wisdom, and music. Throughout his works, William Shakespeare mentions 17 distinct stones of adornment, including agate, amber, carbuncle, chrysolite, coral, crystal, diamond, emerald, flint, jet, lapis lazuli, marble, opal, pearl, ruby, sapphire, turquoise.

AGATE

In Act I, Scene 4 of *Romeo and Juliet*, Mercutio tells of Queen Mab:

"She is the fairies' midwife, and she comes
In shape no bigger than an agate stone
On the forefinger of an alderman."

In Act 3, Scene 1 of *Much Ado About Nothing*, Hero says that

"Nature never framed a woman's heart
Of prouder stuff than that of Beatrice"

who would swear that if a man were tall he would be like

"A lance illheaded;"
"If low, an agate very vilely cut."

In Act 2, Scene 1 of *Love's Labours Lost*, Boyet tells the Princess of France that Navarre's heart is

"Like an agate, with your printed impressed."

In *King Henry IV*, Part I, Act 2, Scene 4, Prince Hal says to Francis:

"Wilt thou rob this leathern jerkin, crystal button, knott-pated,
agate-ring, puke-stocking, caddis-garter, smooth tongue,
Spanish-pouch,..."

Falstaff in Part 2, Act 1, Scene 2, of the same play complains to his page that he was never "manned with an agate till now."
(These quotations all serve to show how popular the agate was as a ring in Shakespeare's time.)

AMBER

Hamlet, in answer to a question, tells Polonius that the "satirical rogue" whose book he is reading says that old men's eyes are "purging thick amber and plum-tree gum" (Act 2, Scene 2), a thought no doubt suggested by the ancient myth of the "weeping sisters."
Petruchio asks his "Mistress Kate":

"Will we return unto thy father's house
With amber bracelets, beads, and all this knavery?"
                    (*Taming of the Shrew*, Act 4)

Says Dumain in *Love's Labours Lost* (Act 4, Scene 3):

"Her amber hair for foul hath amber quoted"

and Biron:

"An amber-coloured raven was well noted."

CARBUNCLE

Dromio of Syracuse in Act 3, Scene 2, of the *Comedy of Errors*, speaks of

"Her nose all o'er embellished with rubies, carbuncles, sapphires."

Titus Lartius says of Marcius:

"Thou art lost, Marcius;
A carbuncle entire, as big as thou art,
Were not so rich a jewel."
Coriolanus, Act 1, Scene 4

Iachimo, the soothsayer, (*Cymbeline*, Act 5, Scene 5) tells that

"He, true knight,
No lesser of her honour confident
Than I did truly find her, stakes this ring:
And would so, had it been a carbuncle
Of Phoebus' wheel, and might so safely, had it
Been all the worth of's car."

Hamlet speaks to the Players (Act 2, Scene 2) of Pyrrhus:

"With eyes like carbuncles, the hellish Pyrrhus
Old grandsire Priam seeks."

Again the poet uses the "carbuncle of Phoebus' wheel" in *Antony and Cleopatra*, Act 4, Scene 8:

"He has deserved it, were it carbuncled
Like holy Phoebus' car."

CHRYSOLITE

The fated Moor says of his poor murdered Desdemona in the last scene of the last act of *Othello*:

"Nay, had she been true,
If Heaven would make me such another world
Of one entire and perfect chrysolite
I'd not have sold her for it."

CORAL

Says Lucentio in Act 1, Scene 1 of *Taming of the Shrew*:

"I saw her coral lips to move
And with her breath she did perfume the air:
Sacred and sweet was all I saw in her."

The charming Ariel in *The Tempest* (Act 1, Scene 2) sings:

"Full fathom five thy father lies:
Of his bones are coral made:
Those are pearls that were his eyes:
Nothing of him that doth fade
But doth suffer a sea-change
into something rich and strange."

CRYSTAL

"But in that crystal scales let there be weighed
Your lady's love against some other maid,"

says Benvolio to Romeo (*Romeo and Juliet*, Act 1, Scene 2).

In *Love's Labours Lost* (Act 2, Scene 1) Boyet tells the Princess of France:

"Me thought all his senses were locked in his eye,
As jewels in crystal for some prince to buy."

In Act 4, Scene 3, of the same play, the King says:

"'Ay, me!' says one: 'O, Jove!' the other cries:
One, her hairs were gold, crystal the other's eyes."

In Act 3, Scene 2 of *A Midsummer Night's Dream*, the awakening Demetrius sings Helen's praises:

"O Helen, goddess, nymph, perfect, divine!
To what, my love, shall I compare thine eyne?
Crystal is muddy."

In Act 2, Scene 1 of *King John*, Queen Eleanor says of the sad sensitive Arthur:

"His mother shames him so, poor boy, he weeps,"

Constance retorting:

"Now shame upon you whether she does or no!
His grandam's wrongs, and not his mother's shames,
Draws those heaven-moving pearls from his poor eyes,
Which Heaven shall take in nature of a fee:
Ay, with these crystal beads Heaven shall be bribed
To do him justice and revenge on you."

Bolingbroke in *Richard II* (Act 1, Scene 1) says:

"Since the more fair and crystal is the sky,
The uglier seem the clouds that in it fly."

Says Bardolph in *Henry V* (Act 2, Scene 3):

"Go clear thy crystals."

At the opening of *King Henry VI*, Bedford has the famous lines:

"Hung be the heavens with black, yield day to night,
Comets, importing change of times and states,
Brandish your crystal tresses in the sky."

In Act 5, Scene 4, of *Cymbeline*, the ghost father Sicilius says:

"Thy crystal window ope: look out."

Two Gentlemen of Verona, Act 2, Scene 4:

"But that his mistress
Did hold his eyes locked in his crystal looks."

The poetic use of crystal has its basis in ancient mystical philosophy, which is partly noticed in the section under Crystal.

DIAMOND

Shakespeare alludes to the diamond 21 times, most of all in *Cymbeline*.

Imogen gives Posthumus as a pledge of affection her diamond ring:

"This diamond was my mother's: take it, heart."

The diamond is mentioned four times as an important part of the plot in the bargain between Posthumus and Iachimo:

"If she went before others I have seen, as that diamond outlusters
many I have beheld, I could not but believe that she excelled many:
but I have not seen the most precious diamond that is, nor you
the lady."

POSTHUMUS: "I praised her as I rated her: so do I my stone."
"I shall but lend my diamond till you return."
IACHIMO: "My ten thousand ducats are yours: so is your diamond too:
if I come off."

In Act 2, Scene 4, poor Posthumus says:

"All is well yet,
Sparkles this stone as it was wont?"

alluding to the ancient belief that the diamond turned dull when lovers proved unfaithful.

". . .The stone's too hard to come by."

IACHIMO: I beg but leave to air this jewel: see! it must be married
To that your diamond."

In Act 5, Scene 5, *Cymbeline* asks Iachimo:

"That diamond upon your finger—say,
How came it yours?"

The diamond is mentioned three times in Pericles:

MAISA: "To me he seems like diamond to glass." (Act 2, Scene 3)
HELICANUS: "Whom if you find, and win unto return,
You shall like diamonds sit about his crown."
CERIMON: "She is alive: behold
Her eyelids, cases to those heavenly jewels
Which Pericles hath lost,
Begin to part their fringes of bright gold:
The diamonds of a most praised water
Do appear, to make the world twice rich."

The diamond is mentioned three times in *King Henry VI*:

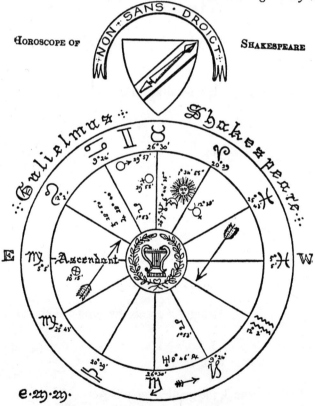

HOROSCOPE OF   SHAKESPEARE

"To me he seems like diamond to glass."
Pericles, Act II, Sc. 3.

KING HENRY: "My crown is in my heart not on my head:
Not decked with diamonds and Indian stones
Nor to be seen: my crown is called content
A crown it is that seldom kings enjoy."
(Part 3, Act 3, Scene 1)

In the *Comedy of Errors*, the diamond is twice mentioned:

THE COURTEZAN: "Give me the ring of mine you had at dinner,
Or for my diamond, the chain you promised."
(Act 4, Scene 3)

THE COURTEZAN: "Sir, I must have that diamond from you."
(Act 5, Scene 1)

In Act 3, Scene 3, in *The Merry Wives of Windsor*, Falstaff says to Mistress Ford:

"I see how thine eye would emulate the diamond."

The Princess in *Love's Labours Lost*, Act 5, Scene 2, speaks of a

"Lady walled about with diamonds."

In *Timon of Athens*, Act 3, Scene 6, the Fourth Lord says:

"One day he gives us diamonds, next dry stones."

In *The Merchant of Venice*, Act 3, Scene 1, Shylock exclaims,

"A diamond gone, cost me two thousand ducats in Frankfurt."

In *Macbeth*, Act 2, Scene 1, Banquo presents the King's diamond with the words:

"This diamond he greets your wife withal."

In *King Lear*, Act 4, Scene 3, the gentleman tells Kent:

"You have seen
Sunshine and rain at once: her smiles and tears
Were like a better way: those happy smilets,

That played on her ripe lip, seemed not to know
What guests were in her eyes: which parted thence
As pearls from diamonds dropped."

EMERALD

Emerald is mentioned but once—in Act 5, Scene 5, of *The Merry Wives of Windsor*, when Mistress Quickly says:

"And 'Honi soit qui mal y pense' write
In emerald tufts, flowers purple, blue and white:
Like sapphire, pearl and rich embroidery
Buckled below fair knighthood's bending knee."

FLINT

Talbot:
"God is our fortress in whose conquering name
Let us resolve to scale their flinty bulwarks."
(*King Henry VI*, Part 1, Act 2, Scene 1)

Gloucester:
"Uneath may she endure the flinty streets."
Duchess of Gloucester:
"The ruthless flint doth out my tender feet."
(*Henry VI*, Part 2, Act 3, Scene 4)

Queen Margaret:
"Because thy flinty heart more hard than they. . ."
(*Henry VI*, Part 2, Act 3, Scene 2)

York (aside):
"Scarce can I speak my choler is so great:
Oh, I could hew up rocks and fight with flint
I am so angry at these abject terms."
(*Henry VI*, Part 2, Act 5, Scene 1)

York:
"Women are soft, mild, pitiful and flexible:
Thou stern, obdurate, flinty, rough, remorseless."
(*Henry VI*, Part 3, Act 1, Scene 4)

Richard:
"Then Clifford were thy heart as hard as steel
As thou hast shown it flinty by they deeds
I come to pierce it or to give thee mine."
(*Henry VI*, Part 3, Act 2, Scene 1)

Lucius:
"Searching the window for a flint I found
This paper, thus sealed up."
(*Julius Caesar*, Act 2, Scene 3)

Brutus:
"O Cassius, you are yoked with a lamb
That carries anger as the flint bears fire."
(*Julius Caesar*, Act 4, Scene 3)

Enobarbus:
"Throw my heart
Against the flint and hardness of my fault."
(*Antony and Cleopatra*, Act 4, Scene 9)

Thersites:
"There were wit in this head, an 'twould out: and so
there is, but it lies a coldly in him as fire in a flint,
which will not show without knocking."
(*Troilus and Cressida*, Act 3, Scene 3)

Demetrius:
"But be your heart to them
As unrelenting flint to drops of rain."
(*Titus Andronieus*, Act 2, Scene 3)

Marcus:
"My heart is not compact of flint nor steel."
(*Titus Andronieus*, Act 5, Scene 3)

Gower:
"Make raging battery upon shores of flint."
(*Pericles*, Act 4, Scene 4)

Poet:
  "The fire i' the flint shows not till it be struck."
  (*Timon of Athens*, Act 1, Scene 1)

Timon:
  "What, dost thou weep? Come nearer. Then I love thee.
  Because thou art a woman and disclaim'st
  Flinty Mankind."
  (*Timon of Athens*, Act 4, Scene 3)

Friar Lawrence:
  "Here comes the lady: oh, so light a foot
  Will ne'er wear out the everlasting flint."
  (*Romeo and Juliet*, Act 2, Scene 6)

Gloucester:
  "I would to God my heart were flint, like Edward's."
  (*Richard III*, Act 1, Scene 3)

Belarius:
  ". . .Weariness
  Can snore upon the flint, when resty sloth
  Finds the down pillow hard."
  (*Cymbeline*, Act 3, Scene 6)

First Priest:
  ". . .For charitable prayers,
  Shards, flints and pebbles should be thrown on her."
  (*Hamlet*, Act 5, Scene 1)

Bastard:
  "Till their soul-fearing clamours have brawled down
  The flinty ribs of this contemptuous city."
  (*King John*, Act 2, Scene 2)

King Richard:
  "Go to Flint castle: there I'll pine away;
  A King, woe's slave, shall kingly woe obey."
  (*Richard II*, Act 3, Scene 2)

Queen:
  "This is the way
  To Julius Caesar's ill-erected tower,
  To whose flint bosom my condemned lord
  Is doomed a prisoner by proud Bolingbroke."
  (*Richard II*, Act 5, Scene 2)

King Richard:
  "How these vain weak nails
  May tear a passage through the flinty ribs
  Of this hard world."
  (*Richard II*, Act 5, Scene 5)

King Henry:
  "He hath a tear for pity and a hand
  Open as day for melting charity:
  Yet notwithstanding, being incens'd, he's flin'"
  (*Henry IV*, Part 2, Act 4, Scene 4)

Othello:
  "The tyrant custom, most grave senators,
  Hath made the flinty and steel couch of war
  My thrice-driven bed of down."
  (*Othello*, Act 1, Scene 3)

Helena:
  "Which gratitude
  Through flinty Tartar's bosom would peep forth,
  And answer 'Thanks.'"
  (*All's Well That Ends Well*, Act 4, Scene 4)

Duke:
  "Pluck commiseration of his state
  From brassy bosoms and rough hearts of flint."
  (*Merchant of Venice*, Act 4, Scene 1)

Viola:
  "My master, not myself, lacks recompense,
  Love make his heart of flint that you shall love;
  And let your fervour like my master's, be
  Placed in contempt! Farewell, fair cruelty."
  (*Twelfth Night*, Act 1, Scene 5)

Holofernes:
"Fire enough for a flint, pearl enough for a swine."
(*Love's Labours Lost*, Act 4, Scene 2)

Volumnia:
"Oh, stand up blest,
Whilst, with no softer cushion than the flint,
I kneel before thee."
(*Coriolanus*, Act 5, Scene 3)

JET

Gloucester: "What colour is my gown of?"
Simpcox: "Black, forsooth: coal black as jet."
King: "Why then, thou know'st what colour jet is of?"
Suffolk: "And yet, I think, jet did he never see."
(*Henry VI*, Part 2, Act 2, Scene 1)

Titus:
"Provide two proper palfreys, black as jet,
To hale they vengeful waggon swift away."
(*Titus Andronicus*, Act 5, Scene 2)

Salarino:
"There is more different between thy flesh and hers than
between jet and ivory."
(*Merchant of Venice*, Act 3, Scene 1)

LAPIS LAZULI

Evans: "What is 'lapis,' William?"
William: "A stone."
Evans: "And what is a 'stone," William?"
William: "A pebble."
Evans: "No, it is 'lapis': I pray you, remember in your prain."
William: Lapis.
Evans: "That is a good William."
(*The Merry Wives of Windsor*, Act 4, Scene 1)

MARBLE

Card. Wolsey:
"When I am forgotten, as I shall do:
And sleep in dull, cold marble."
(*Henry VIII*, Act 3, Scene 2)

King Henry:
"Her tears will pierce into a marble heart."
(*Henry VI*, Part 3, Act 3, Scene 2)

Gloster:
"He plies her hard: and much rain wears the marble."
(*Henry VI*, Part 3, Act 3, Scene 2)

Sicilius: "Peep through thy marble mansion."
Sicilius: "The marble pavement closes."
(*Cymbeline*, Act 5, Scene 4)

Lavinia:
"The milk from her did turn to marble."
(*Titus Andronicus*, Act 2, Scene 3)

Othello:
"Now by yond marble heaven,
In the due reverence of a sacred vow
I here engage my words."
(*Othello*, Act 3, Scene 3)

Hamlet:
"O, answer me! why the sepulchre
Wherein we saw thee quietly inurn'd,
Hath oped his ponderous and marble jaws,
To cast thee up again."
(*Hamlet*, Act 1, Scene 4)

Duke:
"And he, a marble to her tears, is washed with them, but relents not."
(*Measure for Measure*, Act 3, Scene 1)

Mariana:
"Let me in safety raise me from my knees:
Or else forever be confixed here,
A marble monument!"
(*Measure for Measure*, Act 5, Scene 1)

Macbeth:
"I had else been perfect,
Whole as the marble."
(*Macbeth*, Act 3, Scene 4)

3rd Gentleman:
"Who was most marble there, changed colour."
(*The Winter's Tale*, Act 5, Scene 2)

Andriana:
"If voluble and sharp discourse be marred,
Unkindness blunts it more than marble hard."
(*Comedy of Errors*, Act 2, Scene 1)

OPAL

Clown:
"Now, the melancholy god protect thee: and the tailor make thy
doublet of changeable taffeta, for thy mind is very opal."
(*Twelfth Night*, Act 2, Scene 4)

PEARL

Ariel:
"Those are pearls that were his eyes." (See Coral)
(*Tempest*, Act 1, Scene 1)

Macduff:
"I see thee encompass'd with thy kingdom's pearl
That speak my salutation in their minds."
(*Macbeth*, Act 5, Scene 8)

Constance:
"Those heaven-moving pearls." (See Crystal)
(*King John*, Act 2, Scene 1)

Othello:
". . .Of one whose hand,
Like the base Indian, threw a pearl away
Richer than all his tribe."
(*Othello*, Act 5, Scene 2)

King:
"Hamlet, this pearl is thine:
Here's to thy health."
(*Hamlet*, Act 5, Scene 2)

Lear:
"As pearls from diamonds dropped." (See Diamond)
(*King Lear*, Act 4, Scene 3)

Quickly:
"Like sapphire, pearl and rich embroidery." (See Emerald)
(*Merry Wives of Windsor*, Act 5, Scene 5)

Valentine:
"And I, as rich in having such a jewel
As twenty seas, if all their sand were pearl,
The water nectar and the rocks pure gold."
(*Two Gentlemen of Verona*, Act 2, Scene 4)

Proteus:
"A sea of melting pearl which some call tears."
(*Two Gentlemen of Verona*, Act 3, Scene 1)

Proteus:
"But pearls are fair: and the old saying is,
Black men are pearls in beauteous ladies' eyes."
Julia (aside): "'Tis true: such pearls as put out ladies' eyes:
For I had rather wink than look on them."
(*Two Gentlemen of Verona*, Act 5, Scene 2)

Lord:
"Or wilt thou ride? thy horses shall be trapped,
Their harness studded all with gold and pearl."
(*Taming of the Shrew*, Induction, Scene 2)

Gremio:
"In ivory coffers I have stuffed my crowns:
. . .Fine linen, Turkey cushions bossed with pearl."
(*Taming of the Shrew*, Act 2, Scene 1)

Tranio:
"Why, sir, what 'cerns it you if I wear pearl and gold?"
(*Taming of the Shrew*, Act 5, Scene 1)

Touchstone:
"Rich honesty dwells like a miser, sir, in a rich house:
as your pearl in your foul oyster."
(*As You Like It*, Act 5, Scene 4)

Margaret:
"I saw the Duchess of Milan's gown that they praise so. By my troth's
but a night-gown in respect of yours: cloth o' gold, and cuts, and laced
with silver, set with pearls, down sleeves, side sleeves, and skirts,
round underbone with a bluish tinsel."
(*Much Ado About Nothing*, Act 3, Scene 4)

Holofernes:
"Pearl enough for a swine." (See Flint)
(*Love's Labours Lost*, Act 4, Scene 2)

Maria: "This and these pearls to me sent Longaville."
Princess: "What, will you have me or your pearl again?"
(*Love's Labours Lost*, Act 5, Scene 2)

Lysander:
"Tomorrow night when Phoebe doth behold
Her silver visage in the watery glass,
Decking with liquid pearl the bladed glass
A time that lovers' flights doth still conceal,
Through Athens' gates have we devised to steal."
(*A Midsummer Night's Dream*, Act 1, Scene 1)

Fairy:
"I must go seek some dewdrops here
And hang a pearl in every cowslip's ear."
(Act 2, Scene 1)

Oberon:
"And that same dew which sometime on the buds
Was wont to swell like round and orient pearls,
Stood now within the pretty flowerets' eyes."
(Act 4, Scene 1)

Sebastian:
"This is the air: that is the glorious sun:
This pearl she gave me, I do feel't and see't
And though 'tis wonder that enwraps me thus,
Yet 'tis not madness."
(*Twelfth Night*, Act 4, Scene 3)

Falstaff:
"Your brooches, pearls and ouches."
(*Henry IV*, Part 2, Act 2, Scene 4)

King Henry:
"I am a king that find thee, and I know
'Tis not the balm, the sceptre, and the ball,
The sword, the mace, the crown imperial,
The intertissued robe of gold and pearl,
The farced title running 'fore the King,
The throne he sits on nor the tide of pomp
That beats upon the high shore of the world."
(*Henry V*, Act 4, Scene 1)

Clarence:
"Methought I saw a thousand fearful wrecks:
Ten thousand men that fishes gnawed upon:
Wedges of gold, great anchors, heaps of pearl,
Inestimable stones, unvalued jewels,
All scattered in the bottom of the sea:
Some lay in dead men's skulls: and, in those holes
Where eyes did once inhibit, there were crept
As 'twere in scorn of eyes, reflecting gems."
(*King Richard III*, Act 1, Scene 4)

King Richard:
"The liquid drops of tears that you have shed
Shall come again, transformed to orient pearl."
(Act 4, Scene 4)

Cleopatra: "How goes it with my brave Mark Antony?"
Alexas: "Last thing he did, dear Queen,
He kissed—the last of many doubled kisses—
The orient pearl. His speech sticks in my heart."
Cleopatra: "Mine ears must pluck it thence."
Alexas: "'Good friend,' quote he,
'Say the firm Roman to great Egypt sends
This treasure of an oyster.'"
   (*Antony and Cleopatra*, Act 1, Scene 5)

Cleopatra:
   "I'll set thee in a shower of gold and hail
   Rich pearls upon thee."
   (Act 2, Scene 2)

Troilus:
   "Her bed is India: there she lies, a pearl."
   (*Troilus and Cressida*, Act 1, Scene 1)

Troilus:
   "Why, she is a pearl,
   Whose price hath launched above a thousand ships,
   And turned crowned kings to merchants."
   (Act 2, Scene 2)

Aaron:
   "I will be bright and shine in pearl and gold,
   To wait upon this new-made empress."
   (*Titus Andronicus*, Act 2, Scene 1)

Lucius:
   "This is the pearl that pleased your empress' eye,
   And here's the base fruit of his burning lust."
   (Act 5, Scene 1)

RUBY

Fairy:
   "The cowslips tall her pensioners be:
   In their gold coats spots you see:

Those be rubies, fairy favours,
In those freckles live their savours."
(*A Midsummer Night's Dream*, Act 2, Scene 1)

Macbeth:
 "You make me strange
 When now I think you can behold such sights,
 And keep the natural ruby of your cheeks,
 When mine is blanched with fear."
 (*Macbeth*, Act 3, Scene 4)

Mark Antony:
 "Over thy wounds now do I prophesy—
 Which like dumb mouths do ope their ruby lips,
 To beg the voice and utterance of my tongue."
 (*Julius Caeser*, Act 3, Scene 1)

Dromio:
 "Embellished with rubies, carbuncles, sapphires." (See Carbuncle)
 (*Comedy of Errors*, Act 3, Scene 2)

SAPPHIRE

Mistress Quickly:
 "Like sapphire, pearl and rich embroidery." (See Emerald)
 (*Merry Wives of Windsor*, Act 5, Scene 5)

Dromio:
 "Embellished with rubies, carbuncles, sapphires." (See Carbuncle)
 (*Comedy of Errors*, Act 3, Scene 2)

TURQUOISE

Shylock:
 "Thou torturest me, Tubal: it was my turquoise:
 I had it of Leah when I was a bachelor: I would
 not have given it for a wilderness of monkeys."
 (*Merchant of Venice*, Act 3, Scene 1)

UNION

In *Hamlet*, Shakespeare mentions the pearl twice under the name "union."

King: "The King shall drink to Hamlet's better breath;
And in the cup an union shall he throw,
Richer than that which four successive kings
In Denmark's crown have worn."
Hamlet: "Drink off this potion. Is thy union here?"
(Act 5, Scene 2)

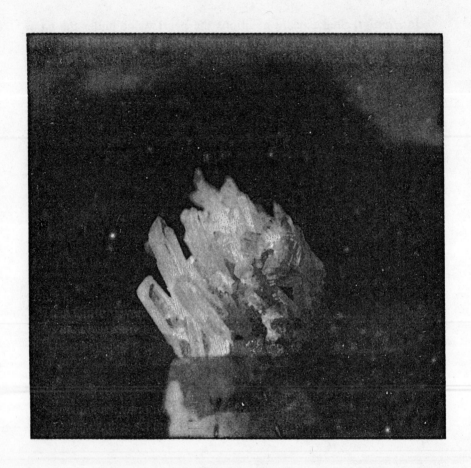

Rhodocrosite

CHAPTER XVI

FORMS, COMPOSITIONS, CHARACTERIS-
TICS, ZODIACAL CLASSIFICATION, AND
PLACES OF ORIGIN

AMBER

Hardness: 2-2.5.
Luster: Resinous.
Chemical Composition: Carbon 78.96, hydrogen 10.51, oxygen 10.52.
Specific Gravity: 1.10-1.13.
Properties: Becomes highly electric by friction. When submitted to heat, organic compounds escape and leave a black residue.
In the Zodiac: Amber is under the heavenly Taurus.
Where Found: Chiefly on the Baltic coast, on the Danish coast, and in parts of Asia.

BERYL
Emerald-Aquamarine

Crystalline System: Hexagonal
Hardness: 7.5-8.
Luster: Vitreous or resinous, transparent to translucent.
Refraction: Weakly double.
Chemical Composition: Silicate of aluminum and beryllium.
Chemical Symbol: $Be3\ A_{l2}\ (SiO_3)C$.
Specific Gravity: 2.63-2.75.
Dichroism: Distinct.
Properties: Exhibits frictional electricity. The emerald clouds before the blowpipe flame without fusing but under intensified heat the edges curve With borax the stone melts into a pale green bead. It resists acids but is affected by microcosmic salt. The stone is so fragile when taken out of the mine that friction crumbles it.
In the Zodiac: All varieties of beryls are under the heavenly Taurus.

Where found: All over the world. Chiefly in Ekaterinburg, Brazil, India, United States, and Australia.

CHRYSOBERYL
Alexandrite-Oriental Chrysolite-Cymophane or Chrysoberyl-Catseye

Crystalline System: Orthorhombic.
Hardness: 8.5.
Luster: Vitreous, transparent to translucent.
Refraction: Double.
Chemical Composition: Alumina 80.2, glucina 19.8.
Chemical Symbol: Be $A_{12}O_{14}$.
Specific Gravity: 3.7-3.86.
Dichroism: Strong in alexandrite, distinct in chrysoberyl.
Properties: Crystals exhibit remarkable twinning at times. Chrysoberyl is highly electric and when submitted to frictional agitation holds electricity for a long time. Not affected by acids. Under the blowpipe it is unaltered and infusible, but it fuses tardily with borax or microcosmic salt. The alexandrite variety which, as Professor J. G. Dana says, bears the same relation to ordinary chrysoberyl as emerald to beryl, displays curious changes of color from leafy green to raspberry red in real and artificial lights.
In the Zodiac: Chrysoberyl is under the heavenly Pisces; alexandrite is under the heavenly Aquarius.
Where Found: Ceylon, Brazil, Russia, Ireland, and Australia.

CORUNDUM
Sapphire, Ruby, Oriental Amethyst, and Oriental Emerald.

Crystalline System: Rhombohedral.
Hardness: 9.
Luster: Transparent to translucent.
Refraction: Moderately double.
Chemical Composition: Aluminum 53-53.2, oxygen 46.8.
Chemical Symbol: Al_2O_3.
Specific Gravity: 3.90-4.16.
Dichroism: Strong.
Properties: Submitted to friction, exhibits electrical properties which withdraw very slowly. Acids do not affect corundum, but under the blowpipe in borax or microcosmic salt it gradually melts to a transparent globule. Radium influences the color strongly, so much indeed as to impart it in achromatic specimens. The stone is variously affected by heat. Treated by

Treated by Sir William Crooks by exposure to high tension electric currents, in a similar way to the diamond, the ruby phosphoresced with an intense red light, and the sapphire with an intense blue.

Dr. T. Coke Squance of Sunderland, well-known in connection with radio-therapeutical research, has succeeded in transforming a faint pink sapphire into a fine ruby. During the process of transformation, the luster of the stone was so intensified that it nearly assumed the brilliancy of a diamond. Dr. Squance observed that both radium and x-rays cause a diamond to glow with a green light. "Besides the diamond," he says, "a mineral called kunzite glows with a lovely red hue. I submitted a sapphire to the radium rays for a long period and it turned to a glorious red. In fact, it had become a ruby. I have similarly transformed other stones, a faint green sapphire, for instance, into an Oriental emerald."

Sir William Crooks noted the sage-green color of the diamond under radium, but found that the color could easily be removed by mechanical means.

In the Zodiac: Blue and green sapphires are under the heavenly Aquarius; white are under the heavenly Pisces; yellow or oriental topaz and rubies are under the heavenly Leo. Oriental amethyst is under the heavenly Sagittarius.

Where Found: Ceylon, China, Burma, Russia, East Indies, United States of America, and Australia (chiefly Queensland).

DIAMOND
Diamond-Boart

Crystalline System: Isometric.
Forms: Octahedron, dodecahedron. Crystals frequently twinned.
Hardness: 10. Scratches every other stone.
Luster: Adamantine. Transparent and, when dark, translucent.
Refraction: Single.
Chemical Composition: Pure carbon.
Chemical Symbol: C.
Specific Gravity: 3.50-3.55.
Properties: Exhibits positive electricity when rubbed, but is itself a non-conductor of electricity. When intensely heated it burns, yielding carbonic anhydride. When heated so as to exclude chemical combination, it dilates and forms into a black concretion. It displays phosphorescence under radium, when submitted to strong sunlight and, when put in a vacuum tube, to a high tension electric current. Dr. G. F. Herbert Smith found that "some diamonds floresce in sunlight, turning milky, and a few emit light when rubbed." Dr. Kunz proved that diamonds phosphoresce when ex-

posed to the rays of radium, polonium, or actinium, even when glass is interposed. These phenomena formed a special object of experiments by the late Sir William Crooks, who showed that, exposed to high tension electric currents in greatly rarified atmosphere, the diamond phosphoresced with an intense green light. Prismatic colors are radiated by this gem.
In the Zodiac: The diamond is under the heavenly Aries, Leo, and Libra.
Where Found: India, Borneo, Brazil, South Africa, Siberia, Australia, and United States of America.

GARNET
Almandine, Pyrope, Hessonite, (Garnet Hyacinth), Uvarovite

Crystalline Form: Isometric.
Hardness: 6.5-7.5.
Luster: Vitreous.
Refraction: Single.
Chemical Composition: Silica alumina, red iron oxide, lime magnesia, manganese, and protoxide.
Chemical Symbol: Dr. Smith has the following formulae:
  Hessonite $Ca_3 Al_2 (SiO_4)3$.
  Pyrope $Mg_3 A_{12} (SiO_4)3$.
    Almandine $Fe_3 A_{12} (SiO_4)3$.
  Andradite $Ca_3 Fe_2 (SiO_4)3$.
Specific Gravity: 3.4-4.3.
Properties: Exhibits positive electricity by friction. With the exception of uvarovite, all varieties of garnets fuse before the blowpipe flame. The stone generally does not contain water.
In the Zodiac: The almandine is under the heavenly Sagittarius; the pyrope, Aquarius; hessonite, Virgo; and uvarovite, Aquarius.
Where Found: All over the world.

OPAL

Crystalline System: None.
Form: Amorphous.
Hardness: 5.5-6.5.
Luster: Waxy to subvitreous.
Refraction: Single.
Chemical Composition: Silica 91.32, water 8.68.
Chemical Symbol: $Si O_2$, $n = Si O_3 n H_2O$.
Specific Gravity: 1.9-2.3
Properties: No electrical properties. Opal exhibits characteristic color re-

flections known as opalescence. It is susceptible to heat and weather changes, exhibiting greater brilliancy on hot than on cold days. The opal has never yet been successfully imitated, and certain peculiar properties remain to be investigated. Professor Frank Rutley F.G.S., emphasizes the fact that "the nature of the Silica (Hydrous Silica) is not yet definitely determined." It is infusible before the blowpipe, but turns opaque.

In the Zodiac: The opal is under the heavenly Leo, Libra, and Aquarius. Leo favors red and fire opal; Libra, light translucent, pure colors, etc.; and Aquarius, dark, black opal.

Where Found: Hungary, Honduras, Mexico, and United States. The finest opal is now found in Australia, principally at Lightning Ridge, White Cliffs, Stuart's Range, and Charleville. (Mr. Conrad H. Sayce gives an analysis of Stuart's Range opal-bearing earth which contains about 35 percent each of alumina and sulphur trioxide. He opines that this may account for the harmful effect it has on the men's eyes and lungs, *Australasian*, March issue, 1920.)

PEARL

Hardness: 3.5-4.
Luster: Translucent.
Chemical Composition: Carbonate of lime and organic matter.
Specific Gravity: 2.65-2.89.
Properties: Affected by acids, benefitted by some skins, adversely affected by others, destroyed by fire.
Where Found: Persian Gulf, Ceylon, Red Sea, South America, New Guinea, Thursday Island, and Australia.
In the Zodiac: Pearls are under the heavenly Cancer.

PERIDOT
Chrysolite-Olivine

Crystalline System: Orthorhombic.
Hardness: 6-7.
Luster: Vitreous, transparent to translucent.
Refraction: Double.
Chemical Composition: Silicate of magnesium and iron.
Chemical Symbol: $(Mg, Fe)2 SiO_4$.
Specific Gravity: 3.3-3.5.
Dichroism: Distinct.
Properties: Friction induces electricity in the stone which is infusible before the blowpipe, but is affected, whitening and forming with borax, a

yellow lead. Decomposes in hydrochloric acid.
In the Zodiac: The peridot is under the heavenly Pisces.
Where Found: United States, Ireland, and Australia, (Queensland particu-
larly). A large number of meterorites contain peridots.

QUARTZ
Rock Crystal, Amethyst, Cairngorm, Chrysoprase, Cat's eye, Plasma,
Jasper, Carnelian, Agate, Onyx, Sardonyx, Moss Agate.

Crystalline System: Rhombohedral.
Hardness: 7.
Luster: Vitreous. Splendent to dull and resinous.
Refraction: Double.
Chemical Composition: Silicon 46.67, oxygen 53.33.
Chemical Symbol: Si O_2.
Specific Gravity: 2.5-2.8. In pure crystals 2.65.
Dichroism: Distinct.
Properties: Generates positive electricity by friction. It is infusible under
the blowpipe, but effervesces with carbonate of soda. Although it resists
the common acids it may be dissolved in hydrofluoric acid.
In the Zodiac: Rock crystal is under the heavenly Pisces; amethyst is
under the heavenly Aries; cairngorm and agate under the heavenly Scorpio;
chrysoprase under the heavenly Cancer; catseye and onyx under the heavenly Capricorn; plasma and jasper under the heavenly Virgo; bloodstone,
carnelian and sardonyx under the heavenly Leo; and moss agate under the
heavenly Taurus.
Where Found: Distributed plentifully about the world. Rock amethyst is
found in the United States, Brazil, India, Ceylon, Ekaterinburg, and Australia. Mr. R. J. Dunn, late Victorian geologist, discovered large quantities
of rose quartz in South Africa. It is also found in the United States, Russia, Australia, and other places. Catseyes are found in Ceylon and India.
Cairngorm is found in Scotland, the United States, and Australia.
Chrysoprase is found in the United States and other places.

SPINEL
Spinel Ruby, Balas Ruby, Rubicelle, Pleonaste or Ceylonite

Crystalline System: Isometric.
Hardness: 8-8 1/2.
Luster: Vitreous.
Refraction: Single.
Chemical Composition: Alumina 72, magnesia 28.

Chemical Symbol: Mg A_{12} O_4.
Specific Gravity: 3.5-4.0.
Dichroism: None.
Properties: Does not display electricity when submitted to friction or heat, but under heat the red spinel changes to brown. On cooling it becomes green, after which it is nearly colorless; then it resumes its pristine hue. Spinel crystals also change into hydrotalcite, a soft pearl-like stone of similar chemical composition. Infusible alone under the blowpipe but yields slowly with borax. It is soluble in concentrated sulphuric acid.
In the Zodiac: Spinel, balas, almandine, ruby, and sapphirine are under the heavenly Virgo. The chloro-spinel and the pleonaste are under the heavenly Capricorn.
Where Found: United States, Canada, Burma, Siam, Ceylon, and Australia. It is discovered in granular limestone, in gneiss and rocks of volcanic origin.

SPODUMENE
Kunzite-Hiddenite

Crystalline Form: Monoclinic.
Hardness: 6.5-7.
Luster: Pearly. Translucent to subtranslucent.
Refraction: Double.
Chemical Composition: Silicate of aluminum and lithium.
Chemical Symbol: Li Al (si O_3)2.
Specific Gravity: 3.5-3.20.
Dichroism: Strong.
Properties: Electrical. Unaffected by acids. Under the blowpipe flame, expands and melts into a clear or opaque glass, indicating lithia by coloring the flame red. Kunzite exhibits phosphorescence under radium.
In the Zodiac: Spodumene and kunzite are under the heavenly Libra. Hiddenite may be under the zodiacal Taurus.
Where Found: United States, Madagascar, Brazil, and Sweden.

TOPAZ

Crystalline Form: Orthorhombic.
Hardness: 8.
Luster: Vitreous. Transparent to translucent.
Refraction: Slightly double.
Chemical Composition: Silicate of aluminum.
Chemical Symbol: [Al $(F_2$ OH)]2 Si O_4. (Penfold and Minor.)

Specific Gravity: 3.4-3.65.
Dichroism: Distinct.
Properties: Becomes strongly electric by friction, heat, and pressure. Infusible alone before the blowpipe flame, but with borax melts into a bead. Changes color when heated.
In the Zodiac: The topaz is under the heavenly Scorpio.
Where Found: Brazil, Ceylon, Mexico, United States, and Australia.

TOURMALINE

Crystalline Form: Rhombohedral.
Hardness: 7-7.5.
Luster: Vitreous.
Refraction: Double.
Chemical Composition: Varied, but all varieties include silicate of alumina, boracic acid, iron, magnesia, lime, and soda, sometimes lithia in small quantity, with fluorine and trace of phosphoric acid.
Chemical Symbol: Professors Penford and Foote refer all varieties of tourmaline to $(H_6 Na_2 Mg_3 A_{l2})3 (A_{l2} Fe)6 (B OH)4 Si_8 O_{38}$.
Specific Gravity: 2.39-3.3.
Dichroism: Strong.
Properties: Becomes charged by heat and friction with positive and negative electricity. Before the blowpipe flame, the darker varieties fuse easily but the lighter more tardily.
In the Zodiac: The tourmaline family is under the heavenly Gemini.
Where Found: Brazil, Russia, California and other parts of the United States, Ceylon, and Australia.

TURQUOISE

Crystalline Form: None.
Hardness: 6.
Luster: Waxy.
Chemical Composition: Dr. Smith gives the composition as a complex phosphate of aluminium, iron, and copper.
Chemical Symbol: Dr. Smith gives Penfold's formula as [Al (OH)2 Fe (OH)2, CU (OH)3 H]3 PO_4, approaching nearly to $H_5 Al_2 PO_6$.
Specific Gravity: 2.6-2.8.
Properties: Infusible before the blowpipe flame, but changes its color to brown. Dissolves in hydrochloric acid. Is affected by acids, oils, and the health of the wearer.
In the Zodiac: Turquoise is under the zodiacal Sagittarius.

Where Found: Chiefly in Persia where the best specimens are found.
Also found in Mexico, Russia, United States, and Australia,.

ZIRCON
Zircon, Jargoon, Hyacinth or Jacinth

Crystalline System: Tetragonal.
Hardness: 7.5.
Luster: Adamantine, transparent to opaque.
Refraction: Strongly double.
Chemical Composition: Silica 33, zirconia 67.
Chemical Symbol: $Zr\,Si\,O_4$.
Specific Gravity: 4.6-4.86.
Properties: Exhibits frictional electricity. The zircon is infusible before the
blowpipe flame, but colored specimens lose their colors. With borax, zircon melts under the blowpipe into a transparent bead. Heated with lime,
the zircon is transformed into a straw-colored stone which so closely resembles the yellow diamond that it is sold to travelers by some unscrupulous Eastern dealers as the more costly gem. Scientists have not yet been
able to explain the constitution and distinct characters of the zircon satis-
factorily.

Professor Sir A. H. Church has made a technical study of the zircon
for over half a century, and is universally accepted as its most authoritative
student. In his researches, he found that in certain varieties of zircon the
green and yellow stones, ground on copper wheel with diamond dust, exhibit a sparkling orange light, and the intermediate golden types radiate orange tints in the flame of a Bunsen burner. Students are seeking for the
unknown element which, blended with zirconium, defies detection. The
zircon is very little affected by acids, except sulfuric acid after very long
steeping. It is also peculiar that, when first heated, the stone exhibits
strong phosphorescence, but as its color leaves it, its specific gravity is
magnified and it will not again phosphoresce when reheated after cooling.
In the Zodiac: All varieties of zircon are under the heavenly Virgo.
Where Found: In almost every part of the world.

Wavelite

CHAPTER XVII

GEMS IN HERALDRY, MAGICAL SQUARES OF ABRA MELIN THE MAGE, CHARUBEL'S GEM INFLUENCES, GEMS OF COUNTRIES

GEMS IN HERALDRY

"Sweet mercy is nobility's true badge."
Titus Andronicus

Without doubt the science of heraldry was evolved from ancient astrological philosophy. Various distinctive badges, shields, and tokens were employed by the peoples of the past, but the system as known today did not properly evolve much before the 13th century. In the present book, that section of heraldry known as "Blazoning by Planets and Precious Stones" deserves some passing notice. By blazoning, the sovereigns and peers were distinguished, the former by the planets and the latter by precious stones, as shown in the following table:

Tincture	Planet	Precious Stone
Or	Sun	Topaz
Argent	Moon	Pearl
Sable	Saturn	Diamond
Gules	Mars	Ruby
Azure	Jupiter	Sapphire
Vertt	Venus	Emerald
Pupure	Mercury	Amethyst
Tenny	Caput Draconis (Moon's North Node)	Jacinth
Sanguine	Cauda Draconis (Moon's South Node)	Sardonyx

The planetary gem grouping is not quite accurate, according to astrological science, and the errors can be referred to the early chroniclers. For example, the ruby is given to Mars and the topaz to the Sun, whereas the ruby is a stone of the Sun and the topaz a stone of Mars. Mars is termed warlike and violent in old works, while the Sun is the emblem of faithfulness and constancy. At the coronation of a British sovereign a ruby ring emblematical of faithfulness and constancy is placed on his finger. Thus it is in harmony with the royal sign Leo, the sign of the Sun, and the monarch who is astrologically ruled by the Sun. The pearl is correct for the Moon; the diamond is not a stone of Saturn; the sapphire is not a stone of Jupiter; the emerald is correct for Venus; and the amethyst is not a stone of Mercury. The assigning of jacinth and sardonyx to the North and South Nodes of the Moon has not the support of astrological science.

MAGICAL SQUARES OF ABRA MELIN THE MAGE

"The wisdom of the Lord is an inexhaustible fountain, neither hath
there ever been a man born who could penetrate its veritable
origin and foundation."

The Second Book of the Sacred Magic

In that remarkable ancient magical work, *The Book of the Sacred Magic of Abra Melin the Mage*, skillfully translated by a past Rosicrucian adept, Monsieur le Comte Macgregor de Glenstrae, are a number of symbolic Name Squares which were variously employed by the old masters who so well knew the use of them. For the finding of certain treasures which are not "magically guarded" ("magically" may here be accepted in a wide sense) the following symbolic power figures were employed:

For **Jewels:** This square, the Comte notes, is a square of 36 squares, and the name "Belial" that of one of the four great chiefs of the evil spirits.

B	E	L	I	A	L
E	B	O	R	U	A
L	O	V	A	R	I
I	R	A	V	O	L
A	V	R	O	B	E
L	A	I	L	E	B

For **Pearls:** A square of 16 squares.

I	A	N	A
A	M	E	N
N	E	M	A
A	N	A	I

For **Diamonds:** A square of 49 squares.

B	I	C	E	L	O	N
I	R	O	L	A	T	O
C	O	R	A	M	A	L
E	L	A	M	A	L	E
L	A	M	A	R	O	C
O	T	A	L	O	R	I
N	O	L	E	C	I	B

For **Rubies:**

S	E	G	O	R
E				
G				
O				E
R			B	S

A border of 12 squares from a square of 25 squares. The Comte translates "Segor" as "to break forth" or "to shut in," according as the root begins with S or Sh.

For **Balassius Rubies:** Twenty squares from a square of 49.

H	E	T	I	S	E	R
E						
T						
I						
S						
E	C	I	N	E	S	E
R						H

For **Emeralds:** A square of 49 squares. "Astarot" is set down in the Comte's notes as one of the eight sub-princes of the evil spirits.

A	S	T	A	R	O	T
S	A	L	I	S	T	O
T	L	A	N	B	S	R
A	I	N	O	N	I	A
R	S	B	N	A	L	T
O	T	S	I	L	A	S
T	O	R	A	T	S	A

To find stolen jewels, the following is given:

K	I	X	A	L	I	S
I	R	I	N	E	Q	I
X						
A						
L				M		
I	Q					
S						K

The square consists of 22 squares taken from a square of 49 squares.

These and many similar figures were used by the Hermetic philosophers in their occult scientific practices. They can be nothing but interesting curiosities to the majority who are ignorant of the trials, sufferings, and disappointments of those brave and faithful Fraters and Sorores who regarded no sin so great as ingratitude and no tendency so foolish as incredulity. "For," says Abra Melin, "you must have faith. Neither should you dispute concerning that which you understand not. God out of nothingness hath created all things, and all things have their being in him. Watch, labour and you will see."

Psychology of Botany, Mineralss, and Precious Stones

In the year 1907, a remarkable book bearing the above title, written by a gifted student who preferred to veil his identity under the pen name of "Charubel," was published by R. Welch, Tyldesley, England. This work is now difficult to obtain. The author insists on a direct sympathy between the human soul and surrounding nature, and his work illustrates his method of linking together these eternal immortal powers so that the human can draw from these elements exactly that force he needs.

The *Psychological Properties of Precious Stones* includes his occult researches into hidden properties which he presents in certain order. The stones mentioned are the topaz, amethyst, coral, rock crystal, emerald, diamond, ruby, turquoise, sapphire, red garnet, carbuncle. "The realm of precious stones," he writes, "abounds with wonders which transcend everything I may have hitherto been made conversant with. Hence, I am very much fascinated with these lustrous specimens of a chemistry which transcends the skill of the ingenious to identify or to produce the same. It is true that so far as appearance goes, modern skill can produce from a kind of paste what resembles the genuine stone, but he can no more produce a living stone than he can make a living tree. The true stone has a life and it is in this life that its true virtue consists."

The virtues of the topaz, writes Charubel, are to be appreciated by "fair people with weak or fragile constitutions, inclined to become despondent, of cold habits. A help to those who are out of sight or in the shade. It begets hopefulness in the hopeless. Strengthens and fortifies the soul against evil, wicked persons." The seal of the topaz is according to our author:

and the sacred name by which it is invoked is Soo-mah-thu-el-di-voo-math-el.

The virtues of the amethyst are set down as a cure for false vision, bad memory, color-blindness, and intoxication.

The seal is given as:

and the sacred name by which the life of the amethyst is invoked is given as Avruthel.

The virtues of the coral, according to Charubel, benefit decrepit persons and those prematurely old. It quickens the senses, is good in defect of the eyesight from gradual loss of energy in the optic nerve, and it strengthens the mental faculties.

The seal is given as:

and the sacred name of invocation Ag-ath-el.

The virtues of the rock crystal include, writes Charubel, safeguard against deception or imposition. "It is for the pure in heart and those who think of a better life."

The seal is given as:

and the sacred name of invocation Ev-ag-el.

The virtues of the emerald are for those "who aspire to wisdom and seek enlightenment, and for those who seek the good of life."

The seal is given as:

and the sacred name of invocation Am-vradel.

The diamond is for "Kings, monarchs, presidents and people of high standing, state authorities and the advanced occultists. The diamond is a gem by the virtue of its homogeneity and belongs to the domain of the true life. The diamond is sacred: one of the most sacred: yes, the most sacred of all gems. I am not allowed to give word and seal for this gem."

Charubel hails the ruby as "the most precious of gems, a balm in the hour of trial, grief, bereavement, disappointment, a soother of agitation and disburdener of the oppressed soul."

The seal of the ruby is given as:

and the sacred word of invocation as Der-gab-el.

The turquoise is set down as the "Sympathetic stone, an invaluable treasure to the thoughtful and meditative, a connector of souls, a developer of Inner Powers."

The seal is given as:

and the sacred word of invocation Har-val-am.

The sapphire is written down as "a cure for doubt and despondency, a reviver of blighted hopes, which robs the future of its dread and renders the Valley of Death redolent with sunshine."

The seal is given as:

and the sacred word of invocation Troo-av-al.

The red garnet is hailed as the stone of inspiration and a remedy for diabolical influences.

The seal is given as:

and the sacred word of invocation as Ar-hu-gal.

The carbuncle "physically strengthens and vivifies the vital and generative forces in human nature, those that lack energy, sufferers from anaemia, and those wanting in animal courage. It sharpens business propensities and is invaluable to the dull, lethargic, sluggish, lymphatic, and people of cold habits."

The seal is given as:

and the sacred word of invocation Aph-ru-el.

GEMS OF COUNTRIES

Old philosophy allots a particular talismanic gem to every country in the world. Those of the following countries are:

Abyssinia: Lapis Lazuli
Afghanistan: Catseye
Albania: Dark Onyx
Algeria: Banded Agate
Arabia: Flint
Argentina: Spodumene
Australia: Opal
Austria: Opal

Bavaria: Topaz
Belgium: Marble
Brazil: Jasper Bloodstone
Bulgaria: Striped Onyx
Burma: Malachite
China: Pearl
Denmark: Hematite
Egypt: Jasper Opal
England: Diamond
France: Ruby
Germany: Hematite
Greece: Dark Onyx
Holland: Pearl
Hungary: Carbuncle
India: Catseye
Ireland: Emerald
Italy: Sardonyx
Japan: Jade
Judea: Topaz
Mexico: Onyx
Morocco: Banded Agate
New Zealand: Nacre
Norway: Topaz
Nubia: Crystal
Palestine: Limonite
Persia: Mocha Stone
Poland: Emerald
Portugal: Chrysolite
Prussia: Sapphire
Rumania: Lapis Lazuli
Russia: Chrysoberyl-Alexandrite
Scotland: Chalcedony
Sicily: Carnelian
South Africa: Pearl
Spain: Turquoise
Syria: Limonite
Sweden: Sapphire
Switzerland: Jasper
Turkey: Jacinth
Transvaal: Cairngorm
United States: Tourmaline
Wales: Marble

CHAPTER XVIII

THE INEVITABLE LAW
OF TRANSMUTATION

"Each change of many colour'd life he drew,
Exhausted worlds and then imagin'd new."
Jonson

Transformation, under the various forms of transfiguration, trans-
mutation, and change, forms the subject of many fascinating stories which
adorn the pages of romance, mythology, science, and symbology. It may
be said to exhibit itself as the dominant force in the world of matter—the
changeful, restless world with which we change and to which, while
dressed in its elements, we are held. The disobedience of Lot's wife
changed her material form into a pillar of salt; the fated Niobe was transformed into a rugged rock which forever was bathed by her tears; the
glance of Medusa turned her victims to stone, her blood turned trees into
coral; the stone which Rhea duped Cronus into swallowing in the belief
that it was one of his children, indeed, the whole legend concerning the
devouring of his offspring by the old god—all illustrate the process of nature which forever consumes that which it produces.

Nature is a veritable alchemist, a royal transmuter, turning the precious
into the base and the base into the precious, regardless of dignity, rank, or
name. Parable and symbol have ever been the ornate coverings beneath
which lie securely hidden from the superficial gaze the secrets with which
searching man has played for ages. The work of these intrepid scientists
had, at certain periods of the world's history, to be carefully concealed
from the vulgar and intolerant mind which was continually endeavoring to
bind the thoughts of men within the slavery of a fixed dogma. The true
meaning of this dogma was indeed far better known and understood by the
faithful searchers into the mysteries of nature than by all the narrow agents
seeking to suppress them. But they were compelled to wait until the
champions of liberty in the material world had swept back the devils of in-
tolerance which darkened the way to spiritual and material freedom.

The waiting for the right time to present their discoveries to the people did not suspend their researches, it rather advanced them. Nearly 600 years before the Christian era, the poetical philosopher Xenophanes wrote of fossil fishes, shells, and other petrifaction found on high mountains and quarries, which he instanced as indicating changes on the earth's surface, certain lands sinking beneath the sea and certain lands rising out of it. The earlier examinations of these remains were considered as evidence of a subtle tractable power inherent in the earth. Plato, Aristotle, and Zeno taught that God entered His Spirit into eternal matter, producing the earth, thus eternally filled with the potential Spirit.

That many-sided genius of the 15th and 16th centuries, Leonardo da Vinci, was rightly regarded by Dmitri Merejkowski as *The Forerunner*, in his historical story of that name. Leonardo was most precise in his remarkable deductions on fossilization, which, he wrote, occurred from the accumulation of mud in the cavities of shells discovered in rivers which were at an ancient period beneath the sea near the coast. Nature's wonderful workings are exhibited in the metamorphoses of the various stones. This process is noticed in the silification of woods, shells, and coral. It is observed in the incrustation of one substance on another. So far as is considered necessary, this subject has been already dealt with.

And so nature is continually proving to man that all is change and that dissolution is impossible. Continually, lower forms are giving place to higher, and the work of the world goes on with the persistent regularity of a huge machine. "Nothing is lost," says chemistry, and even the voice of man, the cries of animals, sounds of breaking rocks, the restless sea, the moaning of the winds amongst the trees, can now be easily impressed on the modern phonograph plates which provide a material working body. Every action can be recorded and reproduced by the photographic camera; even the air can be harnessed to convey a desire. Everything in the Universe, from the stars of Heaven to the atom, or to the minutest subdivision of the atom, is mathematical, law abiding, and under the mysterious and controlling Force which we reverence as God the Infinite.

Nature claims her own, the material goes to the material, "dust to dust," and earth processes turn the visible parts of animals and plants into its identical crystal form. And the controlling powers, about which these perceptible forms materialize, seek the realms of finer forces to which they truly belong. Rightly say the venerable philosophers whose inspired utterances have taught us so much, "The Spirit strips itself to go up and clothes itself to go down."

The writer has tried to make this palpable truth clear in these pages, and trusts that the links in the ancient chain are now left in a little better repair than they were, and that the power within the stone will be better appreciated and better understood. The order of the Infinite Universe is exact and sincere. From its inception the work, trials and struggles of the smallest atom are determined and mind is compelled to express itself. The exact point of union between the visible and the invisible forces has been long known to the hermetic scientists and philosophers whose thoughts are echoed by Wilks, the English poet of *Geology*, in the following lines:

"God is a God of order, though to scan
His works may pose the feeble powers of man."

FINIS

APPENDIX

CONCLUDING REMARKS

It is fascinating to reflect on the progression of events especially in recent years in the study of gemstones since this book was first published in 1922. While Kozminsky obviously had a real feel and appreciation for the healing and spiritual qualities of minerals, many in the gem trade today do not yet have this understanding. Today, with the greatly increased interest in purchasing stones for their healing and consciousness expanding qualities, many in the gem trade have come to appreciate the monetary benefits of appealing to these customers. It is hoped that a deeper understanding of the consciousness stored in gemstones will develop in the future. While interest in quartz crystals currently predominates in the market, the immediate years ahead should demonstrate more interest in many other stones for their metaphysical qualities. This trend is already evident in some conventions. There is also currently little interest in using the actual gem elixirs of stones—the placing of a quality mineral specimen into distilled water under the sun for several hours to transfer the vibrational essence of the stone into the water. In the coming years there will be much more interest in using such elixirs. This will especially develop as people become more sensitive to the energy pattern inherent in gemstones. [1]

1 The gem elixirs are available from Pegasus Products, Inc. P.O. Box 228, Boulder, CO. 80306. (800-527-6104).
Gurudas, *Gem Elixirs and Vibrational Healing,* Vol I (San Rafael, CA: Cassandra Press, 1985).
Gurudas, *Gem Elixirs and Vibrational Healing,* Vol II (San Rafael, CA: Cassandra Press, 1986).